Known Before Birth

By Pieter G.K.M. Bos

PublishAmerica
Baltimore

© 2009 by Pieter G.K.M. Bos.
All rights reserved. No part of this book may be reproduced, stored in a retrieval system or transmitted in any form or by any means without the prior written permission of the publishers, except by a reviewer who may quote brief passages in a review to be printed in a newspaper, magazine or journal.

First printing

PublishAmerica has allowed this work to remain exactly as the author intended, verbatim, without editorial input.

ISBN: 978-1-4489-2467-7 (softcover)
ISBN: 978-1-4489-9067-2 (hardcover)
PUBLISHED BY PUBLISHAMERICA, LLLP
www.publishamerica.com
Baltimore

Printed in the United States of America

With my deepest appreciation to…

My wife and best friend JoAnne. My son and daughter James and Heidi.
To those of the body of Christ, who have been encouragements to us all.
But most of all, my sincere gratitude to our
Heavenly Father who gave His Son, to save the world.

"For God so loved the world that he gave his one and only Son, that whoever believes in him shall not perish but have eternal life. For God did not send his Son into the world to condemn the world, but to save the world through him.–John 3:16-17

*Unless otherwise identified scripture quotations are from the
Holy Bible; New International Version (NIV);
King James Version (NKJV / KJV);
Revised Standard Version of the Bible (RSV).*

"Known before birth"
**Exposing a glimpse of Gods plan for us all, together with
Several significant and practical Christian discipleship principles**

Table of Contents

Introduction 11
1. God's Plan from the Beginning 13
2. A Changed Life 25
3. Being Teachable 39
4. Filled with the Holy Spirit 61
5. Sharing Your Faith 84
6. "Unconditional Surrender" 107
7. Continuing Steadfastly 120
8. Following After Jesus 147
9. A Personal Relationship with Christ 154
10. The Attitude of a Servant 166
11. The Ministry of Giving 175
12. Your Personal Project 185
Conclusion 186
My Closing Thoughts 187
Scripture Index 188
Biography 203

Introduction

From those who are involved in the secular field of psychology, most now acknowledge that all men, no matter who they are, or what they believe, possess the needs to feel safe, and to gain a sense of purpose, significance, love, and fulfillment.

The purpose of this book is to encourage; exhort; educate and empower anyone who is searching for real answers in these important areas of their lives.

This book includes my personal story, how I came from a dysfunctional background; from being an illegitimate child to becoming a "kings kid," and minister. Every chapter shows a different phase of my life, and is followed with several important Biblical principles I learned on the way, on how any person can become the complete person God wants them to be.

1. God's Plan from the Beginning

"...The word of the LORD came to me, saying, "Before I formed you in the womb I knew you, before you were born I set you apart; I appointed you as a prophet to the nations." "Ah, Sovereign LORD," I said, "I do not know how to speak; I am only a child." But the LORD said to me, "Do not say, 'I am only a child.' You must go to everyone I send you to and say whatever I command you. Do not be afraid of them, for I am with you and will rescue you," declares the LORD. Then the LORD reached out his hand and touched my mouth and said to me, "Now, I have put my words in your mouth. See, today I appoint you over nations and kingdoms to uproot and tear down, to destroy and overthrow, to build and to plant."– Jeremiah 1:4-10

Through writing this book, I am hoping to encourage you, challenge you, and motivate you to become all that you could and should be as God placed you in the world we live in.

When God spoke to Jeremiah several thousand years ago, I believe He is communicating to us today the same message. He wants to re-assure us that we are not placed on this earth to walk around lonely or aimlessly. His plan is one of hope and a future. (Jeremiah 29:11).

The Bible say's that God is the potter; we are the clay, and the work of His hand. (Isaiah 64:8) Being the Master Potter, He is affirming us by saying, that he knew why, and what He was doing, long before He made us.

He has placed us on this earth for His purpose. He wanted us!

No matter the circumstances of our birth. We mite have been born and raised in a good family setting, we could be the result of sin in a parent's life, or we could be the victim of a dysfunctional home. Whatever it may be, our sovereign God knew, and wanted us, long before you and I were born.

Jesus said, "You did not choose me, but I chose you and appointed you to go and bear fruit—fruit that will last."–John 15:16

"...He has saved us and called us with a holy calling, not according to our works, but according to His own purpose and grace which was given to us in Christ Jesus before time began..."–2 Timothy 1:9

"...you also, like living stones, are being built into a spiritual house to be a holy priesthood...You are a chosen people, a royal priesthood, a holy nation, a people belonging to God, that you may declare the praises of him who called you out of darkness into his wonderful light."–1 Peter2:5, 9

When God created us, He might have had a different plan for each of us; however His ultimate goal is for each person the same. This is, that our lives might bring glory to His name, and that the world will know Him, as we allow Him to reveal Himself through us. (John 17:4-20)

Because of this, we will never feel totally complete, unless we are somehow involved in living out His purpose.

"For we are God's workmanship...created in Christ Jesus to do good works, which God prepared in advance for us to do."–Ephesians 2:10a.

But before we get into more details about this, I would like to acquaint you with a little bit of my own story, beginning with the family I came from to all that God has taken me through to get me to the present day. I want to give you an opportunity to relate to my experiences, so you will understand the many Biblical principles I learned throughout my life, hoping that you too will reach the victories and breakthroughs you deserve. Or perhaps you could use my story, to encourage someone else.

My story:

I am still an imperfect Christian who is trying to be the person God wants me to be, even though my life has had, and still is faced with many obstacles and challenges. But God has been very good to me. So far, He has sustained me, helped me, protected me and empowered me to overcome them all.

I am the physical result of the fact that my mother was raped in the '50s. Had I been born today I would possibly have been aborted. That is the sad, unfortunate choice of many young mothers in the day we live in, but I grew up under very different circumstances. Being an unwed mother in those early days was tough and often ridiculed, but being the child of one was not easy either. It was as if you carried a label on your forehead, saying "Watch out, here comes trouble!" It was when I was still at kindergarten that I got confronted with the fact that there must be something wrong about me. One morning the teacher asked us what our daddies did for work. As she asked different kids before me, I found out that some of them worked as contractors, factory workers, or were in the military. When she came to me, my response was, "I don't have a daddy." After the teacher started to argue with me, saying that everybody had a daddy and that I was just being rebellious, I got sent home with a note for my mother telling her that she had better straighten me out. The next day my mother brought me to school and had to explain my story. However the first damage had been done.

During those first six years of growing up my grandmother took care of me. Because my mother worked as a maternity nurse for the navy she was often away tending to military families all throughout Holland. When home she busied herself with the church music, playing the organ for many of the services. My grandmother's struggle with diabetes and partial paralysis made it a challenge for her to take care of me. Thus, I was traded off between my uncles and aunts several times; and I even spent time at a children's home. When I was home and they thought I was in need of some "physical encouragement" both my grandmother and my mother were very skilled in using the rug beater on me. When they thought I was just bad they used the wide part, when they thought that I was very bad they used the handle. Personally I felt that I was a very good kid. Well with an exception or two... I remember at one time we visited my aunt and uncle at their house, and in the afternoon, after dinner they put me in one of the guest bedrooms to take a nap. Now keep in mind, I was still about four years old at that time, and just in the morning my aunt had baked three loaves of raisin bread that smelled amazing.

And guess what, when they put me in the guest bedroom to take a nap, I quickly noticed that they had put me in the same room with that freshly baked raisin bread. As I lay there, the aroma wafted down beside my head and I saw that they were still cooling off on the shelves above me. There was no way I could go to sleep.

Now you tell me, how can you, still being a little kid, resist the urge not to take some of those wonderful raisins out of those bread and eat them up?

Of course you can understand, I ended up "paying" for it more then I wanted too.

On Sundays' we attended a traditional Protestant church in The Netherlands. One of those cold imposing structures almost as big as a soccer field, we sat on long wooden benches under four story vaulted ceilings listening to the message as it bounced around bare stone walls. In the back of the church you could see dozens of pipes belonging to the organ in the balcony above. Every Sunday, those pipes came to life and shook the floor beneath us. At Christmas we had great midnight celebrations, with the Salvation Army playing music on their trumpets and drums, and sometimes we even had choirs singing hymns and spiritual songs. The sound in that big building was tremendous. It was as if you were right in the middle of the orchestra. I was baptized in that church when I was still a baby, and close to fifteen years later at this same denomination, I did catechism, and I became a personal member of the church. But having said all that, I had the feeling that the "label" was still there. I felt unwanted, out of place, and without a purpose. This feeling was often enforced by my stepfather and his children who came into my life when I was about 6 years old. Those were challenging, and oppressive times for me…times were I asked myself "why?" Did I matter anything to God? Did God know that I existed? Was I a mistake when I got born? And often, while feeling lonely and misunderstood, I doubted if I was wanted by my family, or if I was even wanted by God.

It wasn't long after my grandmother died, that my mother married a widower with four children: two boys older then me, and two girls younger then me. My stepfather was somewhat of a pragmatist. He believed that it did not matter how he did things, as long as he obtained the result he desired, and he spoke freely that he had absolutely no desire to become a Christian. This resulted not only that my mother was asked by the minister to leave the church because of this unequally yoked relationship, but also that my life was going to change drastically.

He had been renting his house, but my mother had been able to earn enough from the navy, organ playing and church performances to buy her own house. So they moved in with us. Everything that had given me a sense of security went out of the door—literally and figuratively speaking. The first thing my stepfather did was clean house, meaning all our nice handcrafted furniture which had been from my grandmother was thrown out, and cut in pieces to be burned in our backyard. Personally, I believe that when he would have sold it, he could have made a lot of money to take care of the family. After he had destroyed all our furniture, he replaced it with his own more modern looking stuff. Then they made me give up my own bedroom and many of the toys that I called my own were disbursed among my new brothers and sisters who did not treat them with the same care as I had done. Even the watch my grandmother gave me just before she died moved to the wrists of one of them who communicated to his father that mine was better then his. After a short while I even ended up losing my friends to my step brothers and step sisters who somehow knew how to convince them that I was not as much fun to play with as they were. Of course, when you're a kid, having a pocketful of candy to share helps a lot. And when something bad had happened, it was easy for them to point their fingers at me.

There was so much to deal with in my new family life that soon enough I was spending more time on the street than at home. I was not yet seven years old that I started to look for ways to earn some money and be independent. Den Helder, the town I lived in, is a harbor town on the northern seacoast of the Netherlands. After asking around and strolling the docks I learned that the fish hall was looking for help on Fridays and Saturdays. It was there alongside the bobbing fishing boats that thronged into the harbor that I spent every free chance I had, helping out and making money. Many times the men at the docks would give me fish of my own to take home and share with the family.

Doing this I was hoping that I would be valued, and accepted more than I felt I was. But even this ended up a disaster in the fact that my stepfather saw this as me competing with him and his children. It was during one of the hot summer days we had, that my stepfather made a comment that I was unproductive and worthless. To defend myself I reminded him about the many bags of fish I had brought home. This made him so mad that he began yelling aggressively that he didn't care about them while he threw out all the fish we had stored in the freezer into the middle of the back yard where they would melt and go bad in the sun.

Later that year, I had an accident with my bike and ended up falling into the harbor. Because I was fully dressed in heavy rubber boots and a thick wool jacket, swimming was nearly impossible. Not only that, but the dock was ten feet above me and the cold water could have given me hypothermia. I should have been crushed by the ship that was tied to the dock and drowned. Yet my father was more concerned about what had had happened to the bike than what had happened to me or even how I had ever made it out of the water.

Enduring events like this for years wore on me. When I became a teenager, I felt like wanting to get away from everything, hoping for something better. As soon as I had finished school, I left my home and became a sailor aboard a cargo ship. I did this for about two and a half years, on a ship traveling mostly from the coast of Africa, all the way to the countries surrounding the Baltic Sea and back. However, though I had been to church, doing all the required stuff, there was still something missing in my life. It was on one dark night, having left the shores of Finland in the early afternoon that day before that I found my self in big trouble. We were still at the Baltic Sea. A sea known for their treacherous storms, as many ships had found there their final resting place in the past. It was when the ship started to hit the big waves with its bow that our cargo started to move from the rear of the ship to the front of the ship, lifting the propeller and the rudder out of the water. Normally cargo dividers would have kept everything in place, but because we had forgotten to put them in, the cargo could move were it wanted. It was being in this kind of trouble that I finally found out what was lacking in my life.

Throughout the years of going to church, and Sunday school, I learned a lot about God, but I never learned to really know God. I had faithfully memorized scriptures when required, and was trying to obey the Ten Commandments, but I had become religious. I had become a "denominational" Christian without having a relationship with Jesus. For me, the Bible was a great history book with some wonderful stories, but I could not relate to it. I believed in God, but felt far removed from Him. I believed I was going to heaven when I would die, but that was only because the preacher had told me so, and because that this was the thing I wanted to believe.

In that storm, on board of that ship, fearing the worst, I came to the realization that I was not only physically in trouble; spiritually I was in much worse straits. In desperation, I found my little pocket Bible buried in the bottom of bags. Very fortunately for me, someone had thought to give it to me prior to my sailors' adventure. Waves beat the sides of the ship violently and torrents of wind hurled rain hard against the deck. Panicked, I flipped the pages, but as the Bible had never really made sense to me before I had no idea what to look for. I started to cry out to God.

Somehow I knew that even though I had fulfilled all the requirements given by the church, when I was going to drown in that ocean, or die on board of that ship, I would not only become fish food, but I would go to Hell. Yes, I had called myself a Christian, but personally I had never really made the choice to be wholly devoted in my living for Jesus. The ironic part of all this is, I knew that when I was still a child, I was called to serve Him. I had even dared to dream that when I would be a little older, I would work at one of the mission ships operated by Operation Mobilization. But instead, without being aware of it I had become like one of those people talked about in the book of Matthew, where Jesus said:

"These people honor me with their lips, but their hearts are far from me. They worship me in vain; their teachings are but rules taught by men." –Matthew 15:8-9

It was then, when I started to cry out to God from my heart that things became clear to me and I felt God speaking. I had allowed my environment to rule me, blaming everybody else for my circumstances and most of all; I had never surrendered my life to Jesus. I had run away from my problems, rather then taking responsibility for my own life and the choices I had made.

My prayer was something like this:

"Lord when you really exist, and when you love me, please HELP! Please forgive me of my sins. Save me, and I promise to live for you the rest of my life."

It was at that night that my life started to change. I had my first encounter with a loving, merciful God, who forgave my sin, and filled me with the Holy Spirit, and with a peace I never knew existed. I learned I was not a mistake. I was wanted and had a reason for being alive.

From that time on my life changed from being without a goal and purpose, to being fulfilled. I learned that I was loved unconditionally. It was the beginning of my adventure with God, and my start in doing those things I know I am called to do. Living for Jesus—Becoming like Jesus—Being a disciple of Jesus, making Disciples, while looking forward to an eternity spent in the presence of The King of King's and Lord of Lords.

During the years following this experience, the Bible taught me that:

Before we were formed in the womb he knew us, before we were born He had set us apart; He has appointed us as representatives to the nations, and we are told go to everyone He sends us too, and say whatever He commands of us. It does not matter how we came to existence, God knew us and wanted us—even though we might not have come the way He would have liked it to be. Even now, when you read this book, you might have made some bad choices, and taken some wrong turns in the past. I want you to know that you are not a stranger to Him. He knows you! You are important to Him! You are wanted by Him,

And this is my covenant with them when I take away their sins." As far as the gospel is concerned, they are enemies on your account; but as far as election is concerned, they are loved on account of the patriarchs, for God's gifts and his call are irrevocable.–Romans 11:27-29

God wants us to become imitators of Jesus in ALL aspects of our life, while enjoying all of His promises. This means that we are to live by the words of Jesus, and to open our lives to the Holy Spirit for our transformation, to become more and more like Him—Enjoying the live he has planned for us. When you allow Him, He will help you!

Jesus said: *The thief comes only to steal and kill and destroy; I have come that they may have life, and have it to the full.–John 10:10*

Life can be tough sometimes

When you have read my story, you might think, "Where is God in all of this"?
Attempting to shine some light on this question, I believe it is important to remember that our creator, the Father of all that is good is opposed by the father of all that is evil. What our common enemy has done throughout the years, he will continue to do so until the return of Christ. Whatever God is creating, the devil will try to kill it, steal it, or destroy it. (John 10:10a)

The Apostle Paul wrote about this in Ephesians 6:12, 13 where he said,
"For our struggle is not against flesh and blood, but against the rulers, against the authorities, against the powers of this dark world and against the spiritual forces of evil in the heavenly realms." Therefore put on the full armor of God, so that when the day of evil comes, you may be able to stand your ground..."

This means for us, that we can make the choice to let evil have its final word in our lives, or, we can choose to have the attitude of Joseph. (Read: Genesis 30:22–50:26)

He was a godly man, but because he was sold out by his brothers, he had to overcome a series of un-fair challenges. Choosing to remain faithful to God in the midst of his trails, God raised him up to save his own people. When finally all of his brother's evil deeds against him had been exposed, he told them: *"You intended to harm me, but God intended it for good to accomplish what is now being done, the saving of many lives."–Genesis 50:20.*

Saying this did not mean that he was justifying his brother's behavior, but looking at the end result, he recognized the preparation process he had to go through, that caused him to be able to fulfill God's ultimate plan.

The reality of life is that we all will have our own valleys to go through, but with the help of God, and by maintaining the right attitude in the midst of it all, we will ultimately experience a great victory. For this is God's desire for us (Read: Psalm 23).

Looking forward, while remembering the past, I can appreciate the words found in King David's prayer, *"... Turn to me and have mercy on me, as you always do to those who love your name. Direct my footsteps according to your word; let no sin rule over me. Redeem me from the oppression of men, that I may obey your precepts. Make your face shine upon your servant and teach me your decrees..."–Psalm 119:132-135*

Value close relationships

All Christians are like the twelve disciples, called to live in close relationship, first of all with Jesus, and then in close relationship with one another. He wants to love you, and have His love flow through you!

We are to live by the words of Jesus, and to open our lives to the Holy Spirit for our transformation, to become more and more like Jesus, being Christ's disciples…, Making disciples for Christ. When you yield to Him, He will help you, empower you, and use you!

As you sent me into the world, I have sent them into the world. For them I sanctify myself, that they too may be truly sanctified. "My prayer is not for them alone. I pray also for those who will believe in me through their message, that all of them may be one, Father, just as you are in me and I am in you. May they also be in us so that the world may believe that you have sent Me. I have given them the glory that you gave me, that they may be one as we are one: I in them and you in me. May they be brought to complete unity to let the world know that you sent me and have loved them even as you have loved Me.–JESUS (John 17:18-23)

As you have started to read the beginning of my story, perhaps you have related to some of the things I wrote so far. When that is through, I want to begin with assuring you that God has a plan for you! And when you are wondering about the purpose of your life, longing for security, significance, love and fulfillment, I want you to know that God wants to meet those needs.

KNOWN BEFORE BIRTH

Now to him who is able to do immeasurably more than all we ask or imagine, according to his power that is at work within us, to him be glory in the church and in Christ Jesus throughout all generations, for ever and ever! Amen.–Ephesians 3:20, 21

When you are already a Christian, and have been exposed to the Great Commandment to make disciples and wanting to be obedient to it, you might ask yourself, "How do I know what a disciple looks like?" Or, "Am I good enough, even after all the mistakes I have made in the past?"

I want to remind you, Jesus Christ wants all of us to follow Him and He can and wants to use us no matter what our background, talents or abilities are. Just look at His first 12 disciples. They had some shady backgrounds and made some mammoth mistakes. The big question is, "Are we willing?" "Do we love Jesus enough to do whatever He asks us to do or go where ever He sends us?" That is what makes the difference between being a disciple of Jesus Christ or not.

God knows we are not perfect. We can all try to hide behind the excuse that we will never be perfect in our lifetime. However, this is never acceptable evidence or reason enough to not try to be what God wants us to be as we use the tools and direction God has given us to get the job done.

Before Jesus went up to heaven Jesus gathered His disciples around Him and stated:

"All authority in Heaven and on earth has been given to me. Therefore, go and make disciples of all nations, baptizing them in the name of the Father, and of the Son, and of the Holy Spirit, and teach them (instructing / disciple) to obey everything I have commanded you, and surely I will be with you always, to the very end of the age.–Matt.28:18-20.

In Mark 16:17, we can read that signs and wonders follow those who believe.

Once when large crowds of people were going along with Jesus, he turned and said to them "Whoever comes to me cannot be my disciple unless he loves me more than he loves his father and his mother, his wife and his children, his brothers and his sisters and himself as well. Whoever does not carry his own cross and come after me cannot be my disciple. vs. [33] "In the same way," concluded Jesus "none of you can be my disciple unless he gives up everything he has."–Luke 14:25-27, 33;

The Apostle Paul wrote:

"Therefore, if anyone is in Christ, he is a new creation; the old has gone, the new has come! All this is from God, who reconciled us to himself through Christ and gave us the ministry of reconciliation: that God was reconciling the world to himself in Christ, not counting men's sins against them. And he has committed to us the message of reconciliation. We are therefore Christ's ambassadors, as though God were making his appeal through us. We implore you on Christ's behalf: Be reconciled to God."
–2 Corinthians 5:17-20

2. A Changed Life

So I tell you this, and insist on it in the Lord, that you must no longer live as the Gentiles do, in the futility of their thinking. They are darkened in their understanding and separated from the life of God because of the ignorance that is in them due to the hardening of their hearts.–Ephesians 4:17, 18

Even before that first spiritual experience where I cried out to God in the storm I was aware without any shadow of doubt that my life was filled with mistakes. But when I finally met God the feeling I had became so much more intense, that you could almost compare it to the experience Isaiah had as described in Isaiah 6:5: *"Woe to me!" I cried. "I am ruined! For I am a man of unclean lips, and I live among a people of unclean lips, and my eyes have seen the King, the LORD Almighty."* I think that when he would have spoken like Americans, he might have said something like, "O boy, I am in deep trouble, I have so much sin in my life, I am sure God is going to kill me." I do not want to boast on my sinfulness, but like him, I needed mercy and forgiveness. I needed to start over again with a clean slate. I needed to change my focus, my behavior and my life. This perhaps emotional—holy experience brought me to my knees, and led me to asking for forgiveness, and another chance for my life.

In the book of Acts, we can see another example of holy conviction taking place.

The Apostle Peter, on the day of Pentecost said to those who desperately wanted to know how to get into a right relation with God:

"Repent and be baptized, every one of you, in the name of Jesus Christ for the forgiveness of your sins. And you will receive the gift of the Holy

Spirit. The promise is for you and your children and for all who are far off—for all whom the Lord our God will call." With many other words he warned them; and he pleaded with them, "Save yourselves from this corrupt generation." Those who accepted his message were baptized, and about three thousand were added to their number that day.–Acts 2:28-41

Peter started his message with, the word "Repent." Because it is sin that separates us from God. The Psalmist wrote,
"If I regard iniquity in my heart, the Lord will not hear me"–Psalm 66:18

But what does repentance mean?

To repent means to turn around, go in the opposite direction, or to change your course. Repentance results in a drastic change in someone's life. "Just as you used to offer the parts of your body in slavery to impurity and to increasing wickedness, now surrender them to righteousness leading to holiness"–Romans 6:19. Paul is saying in effect, "Just as you went headlong into sin with complete dedication, never thinking anything about it, now repent and use that same degree of dedication to go toward righteousness and holiness." From living to please you're self, to living to please God. Through repentance is not only feeling sorry, or to stop doing the wrong we did, but also a start of the good we know we are called to do. We repent of our sins and turn to God. The Apostle Paul said: *"Flee from sexual immorality. All other sins a man commits are outside his body, but he who sins sexually sins against his own body. Do you not know that your body is a temple of the Holy Spirit, who is in you, whom you have received from God? You are not your own; you were bought at a price. Therefore honor God with your body."– 1 Corinthians 6:18-20*. Paul also wrote: *"Therefore come out from them and be separate,' says the Lord. 'Touch no unclean thing, and I will receive you"–2 Corinthians 6:17.*

Getting rid of our "grave clothes."

Perhaps you remember the story of Lazarus (John 11:17-44). I believe that this is a great story of someone who was dead, and was brought back to life. Just as we were dead in our sin before we accepted Jesus into our life and, and were brought to life because of the work of Jesus on the cross. *(I think that this is a great example of evangelism and discipleship in motion).*

Lazarus was a friend of Jesus, but had died and was buried for four days before Jesus arrived at the place where he was laid to rest. When Jesus came, He told the disciples to roll the stone of the grave away. At that moment the people who were there were quick to remind Him that that was not a good idea. "His body smelled" they said. Notice what happened. First Jesus had to deal with some controversy from people who could not see the benefit from His demands. Jesus then prayed (vs.41), and started to call out the name of Lazarus (vs.43), with the result that Lazarus woke up and came outside. However, when he came out of his grave it say's: *(Vs. 44) the dead man came out, his hands and feet wrapped with strips of linen, and a cloth around his face. Jesus said to them, "Take off the grave clothes and let him go." (vs.45) Therefore many of the Jews who had come to visit Mary, and had seen what Jesus did put their faith in him.*

To summarize what had happened:

When we are planning to change our lifestyle, we mite experience some controversy. We will experience an inward struggle against changing that what we know needs to change. And we might not have the positive encouragement from our environment we need.

Lazarus had seen the light. He heard words of truth. *(Evangelism)* And he had heard the voice of Jesus calling his name. The message was a personal message to him.

All of this was followed by the fact that Lazarus responded to the call. However, when he came out of the tomb, was still bound up with grave clothes. He was made alive, but the bondages and the smell of death were still present. At that time Jesus told those who were witnessing this miracle to take off the grave clothes and let him go." *(Discipleship in action)* This is the time where we are confronted with our sin and our sinfulness. We need to repent, and get rid of anything that mite separate us from the presence of God.

But if we walk in the light, as he is in the light, we have fellowship one with another, and the blood of Jesus Christ his Son cleanses us from all sin. If we say that we have no sin, we deceive ourselves, and the truth is not in us. If we confess our sins, he is faithful and just to forgive us our sins, and to cleanse us from all unrighteousness. If we say that we have not sinned, we make him a liar, and his word is not in us.–1 John 1:7-10

Let's examine some of our grave clothes.

Our way of thinking

Therefore, I urge you, brothers, in view of God's mercy, to offer your bodies as living sacrifices, holy and pleasing to God—this is your spiritual act of worship. Do not conform any longer to the pattern of this world, but be transformed by the renewing of your mind. Then you will be able to test and approve what God's will is—his good, pleasing and perfect will.–Romans 12:1,2.

During our counseling sessions with some of the students we have had, I have often made the comment, that when you feed your self with the negative; you often end up feeling the same way. This then could result in to negative behavior. However when you feed your self with the positive, you will feel good, resulting that you also will behave positive.

The Bible teaches us that we need to learn to change our mind. From being negative and hopeless in our thinking, we need to become hopeful and positive thinkers. In stead of thinking that every one is against you, or out to get you, we need to start believing that God is for us, and not against us. God does not look down upon you, but has a divine plan and future for us (Jeremiah 29:11). That means we need to change and protect our mind from the things of the world. We do that by guarding our mind from negative influences. Like the television, the radio, the music we listen to, the books and magazines we read. A good rule of thumb could be reasoning that whatever it is you are looking at, or listening too, when it is not good enough for Jesus, it is not good enough for you. .

Finally, brothers, whatever is true, whatever is noble, whatever is right, whatever is pure, whatever is lovely, whatever is admirable—if anything is excellent or praiseworthy—think about such things.– Philippians 4:8

Our Attitudes

Repentance means a change of attitude. We must have a change of attitude about God. We must have a change of attitude about sin in our own life. It is no longer something to be played with, but is a transgression against a holy God. We must consciously separate our self from sin. We must have a change of attitude about salvation; we must realize that it is God who saved us and not we ourselves, *"it is by grace through faith."–Ephesians 2:8, 9.*

We must also change our attitudes about daily issues we face in life, such as cheating in school or what we watch on TV and our relationships with those closest to us, especially family and friends. All should be affected by our recognition of God's desire for us to live a pure and holy life. Sensitivity to the Holy Spirit in these areas will help us live a pure life.

Our Desires

"Set your minds on things above, not on earthly things"–Colossians 3:2

When a person is outside of Christ, the desires that motivate him are possessions, fame, or creating a reputation, which the world looks up too. In our culture we have millions of people rich and poor alike who are preoccupied with materialism. People are concerned with what others think of them. Many are concerned solely with self and the pleasure they can get out of life. Those selfish ambitions should change when a person comes to Christ. Before salvation we are not interested in the ways of God; we do not care about the Bible. We don't want to go to church or be associated with other Christians. But all that should change and our new desires should be directed toward God and everything concerning him.

Our past experience.

And Jesus said unto him, "No man, having put his hand to the plow, and looking back, is fit for the kingdom of God."–Luke 9:62

We want to go forwards, but we are still looking back. We are not sure we want to leave our old life of sin at the altar. Perhaps you too have experienced so many disappointments and hurts that you can't look at the future without thinking about the past—expecting the worst. You say you want to do better, but you are always copying previous behavior patterns.

Have you ever tried to run forward while looking over your shoulder? You know that by doing that, it is asking for an accident to happen. Speaking from personal experience, I know this to be the truth. Now over thirty years later, I can still be influenced by negative things that had happened in the past, and have to make the conscious choice to look forwards and upwards. .

The Apostle Paul said about himself: *"Not that I have already obtained all this, or have already been made perfect, but I press on to take hold of that for which Christ Jesus took hold of me. Brothers, I do not consider myself yet to have taken hold of it. But one thing I do: Forgetting what is behind and straining toward what is ahead, I press on toward the goal to win the prize for which God has called me heavenward in Christ Jesus."–Philippians 2:12-14*

Our Sin

As obedient children, do not conform to the evil desires you had when you lived in ignorance. But just as he who called you is holy, so be holy in all you do; for it is written: "Be holy, because I am holy."–1 Peter 1:14-16

As a result of the Holy Spirit's taking up residence within us, a deep sensitivity to sin will rise up within us. Meaning, that when we submit ourselves to the leading of the Holy Spirit, and commit ourselves to the full authority of God's will and His Word. we will want to make the voluntary choice to avoid every form of evil. King Solomon said this of the righteous person's attitude toward sin: *"To fear the Lord is to hate evil; I hate pride and arrogance, evil behavior and perverse speech"–Proverbs 8:13.*

Our Old Influences

But mark this: There will be terrible times in the last days. People will be lovers of themselves, lovers of money, boastful, proud, abusive, disobedient to their parents, ungrateful, unholy, without love, unforgiving, slanderous, without self-control, brutal, not lovers of the good, treacherous, rash, conceited, lovers of pleasure rather than lovers of God—having a form of godliness but denying its power. Have nothing to do with them.–2 Timothy 3:1-5

One other evidence of repentance is that old influences, which often would lead us astray, are broken off. And this is hard to do because it involves people. In some cases, when we continue to associate with the "old crowd," they may drag us down. We may have to make a clean break.

As we grow in our knowledge of Christ, our circle of friends should include more and more Christians. God does not want us to drop all our non-Christian relationships altogether, but he certainly wants us to drop out of the things they do that would draw us back toward sin. We need to minister the gospel to the sinner, but not participate in any of their sinful activities.

God's standard for us:

Therefore, prepare your minds for action; be self-controlled; set your hope fully on the grace to be given you when Jesus Christ is revealed. As obedient children, do not conform to the evil desires you had when you lived in ignorance. But just as he who called you is holy, so be holy in all you do; for it is written: "Be holy, because I am holy." Since you call on a Father who judges each man's work impartially, live your lives as strangers here in reverent fear.–1 Peter 1:13-17

Now that you have purified yourselves by obeying the truth so that you have sincere love for your brothers, love one another deeply, from the heart. For you have been born again, not of perishable seed, but of imperishable, through the living and enduring word of God.–1 Peter 1:22-23

The Biblical standards for purity that God desires from us are:

We are to live by the Spirit

The Apostle Paul wrote, *"Since we have these promises, dear friends, let us purify ourselves from everything that contaminates body and spirit, perfecting holiness out of reverence for God"–2 Corinthians 7:1.*

So I say, live by the Spirit, and you will not gratify the desires of the sinful nature. For the sinful nature desires what is contrary to the Spirit and the Spirit what is contrary to the sinful nature. They are in conflict with each other, so that you do not do what you want. But if you are led by the Spirit, you are not under law. The acts of the sinful nature are obvious: sexual immorality, impurity and debauchery; idolatry and witchcraft; hatred, discord, jealousy, fits of rage, selfish ambition, dissensions, factions and envy; drunkenness, orgies, and the like. I warn you, as I did before, that those who live like this will not inherit the kingdom of God. But the fruit of the Spirit is love, joy, peace, patience, kindness, goodness, faithfulness, gentleness and self-control. Against such things there is no law. Those who belong to Christ Jesus have crucified the sinful nature with its passions and desires. Since we live by the Spirit, let us keep in step with the Spirit.–Galatians 5:16-25

Paul cautioned the Ephesians. *"And do not grieve the Holy Spirit of God, with whom you were sealed for the day of redemption"–Ephesians 4:30.*

The Apostle Peter reminds us: *"His divine power has given us everything we need for life and godliness through our knowledge of him who called us by his own glory and goodness. Through these he has given us his very great and precious promises, so that through them you may participate in the divine nature and escape the corruption in the world caused by evil desires. For this very reason, make every effort to add to your faith goodness; and to goodness, knowledge; and to knowledge, self-control; and to self-control, perseverance; and to perseverance, godliness; and to godliness, brotherly kindness; and to brotherly kindness, love. For if you possess these qualities in increasing measure, they will keep you from being ineffective and unproductive in your knowledge of our Lord Jesus Christ. But if anyone does not have them, he is nearsighted and blind."–2 Peter 1:3-9*

So God asks us to be sensitive in our own spirit and depend on His words and promises, that we might remain pure and His Holy Spirit might change us from the inside out. Then we can become Holy as He is Holy.

"'Consecrate yourselves and be holy, because I am the LORD your God. Keep my decrees and follow them. I am the LORD, who makes you holy.–Leviticus 20:7-8

Purity in body

Do you not know that your body is a temple of the Holy Spirit, who is in you, whom you have received from God? You are not your own; you were bought at a price. Therefore honor God with your body.–1 Corinthians 6:19-20

If our mind is under the control of the Holy Spirit, it will make it easier for us to keep our body pure. But we must still work hard at it nevertheless because temptations will surely come, particularly in this sensually oriented culture. Paul spoke to this issue when he wrote, *"It is God's will that you should be holy; that you should avoid sexual immorality; that each of you should learn to control his own body in a way that is holy and honorable, not in passionate lust like the heathen, who do not know God"–1 Thessalonians 4:3-5.*

God wants his people to conduct themselves in such a way that their bodies are pure and clean.

Purity in our thoughts

Paul wrote to the Corinthians, who were surrounded by temptations of impurity,:

The weapons we fight with are not the weapons of the world. On the contrary, they have divine power to demolish strongholds. We demolish arguments and every pretension that sets itself up against the knowledge of God, and we take captive every thought to make it obedient to Christ– 2 Corinthians 10:4-5.

One of the worst things a Christian can do is to start thinking and feeding himself by daydreaming about impure things. Job is an example of what we must do. He said, "I made a covenant with my eyes not to look lustfully at a girl"–Job 31:1.

Purity in our speech

"Nor should there be obscenity, foolish talk or coarse joking, which are out of place, but rather thanksgiving"–Ephesians 5:4.
The Apostle Paul warned, *"Do not let any unwholesome talk come out of your mouths, but only what is helpful for building others up according to their needs, that it may benefit those who listen"–Ephesians 4:29.*

We are to seek purity in our speech. Questionable jokes or stories should not be part of the Christian's conversation. In other words, we ought to think before we speak; when we think, many of the things we usually say would never pass our lips because we would realize that they are not always thoughtful, truthful, and pure.

Purity in our relationships

Paul challenged the Ephesians with these words:
Therefore each of you must put off falsehood and speak truthfully to his neighbor, for we are all members of one body. "In your anger do not sin": Do not let the sun go down while you are still angry, and do not give the devil a foothold. He who has been stealing must steal no longer, but must work, doing something useful with his own hands, that he may have something to share with those in need. Get rid of all bitterness, rage and anger, brawling and slander, along with every form of malice. Be kind and compassionate to one another, forgiving each other, just as in Christ God forgave you–Ephesians 4:25-28, 31-32.

We need to be sensitive to the Spirit of God and to his leading in the way we handle our self with people, and we should follow the teaching of Jesus when he said, "Let your light shine before men, that they may see your good deeds and praise your Father in heaven"–Matthew 5:16.

Solomon also said, "*A man of many companions may come to ruin, but there is a friend who sticks closer than a brother*"–Proverbs 18:24. One honest, caring friend is more valuable than many casual acquaintances. Our relationships with our family and friends must be based on purity. We need each other, for as the Bible says, "As iron sharpens iron, so one man sharpens another" (Proverbs 27:17). Real friendships result from sharing our life with other people. Part of our responsibility as a friend is accepting and giving encouragement, exhortation and sometimes even correction. It is by this means that we are able to help one another withstand temptation and remain pure. The battle for purity is a matter of choice, a matter of obedience to God, a matter of commitment to HIM to live his way. But when we do fall, we need to recognize that we have sinned, then confess it immediately and seek God's forgiveness. We can then know that the sin is forgiven, our life is cleansed, and that God accepts us on the basis of the finished work of Jesus Christ on the cross of Calvary.

Dear friends, I urge you, as aliens and strangers in the world, to abstain from sinful desires, which war against your soul. Live such good lives among the pagans that, though they accuse you of doing wrong, they may see your good deeds and glorify God on the day he visits us–1 Peter 2:11-12.

To summarize it in the words of the Apostle Paul:

"Flee the evil desires of youth, and pursue righteousness, faith, love and peace, along with those who call on the Lord out of a pure heart."–2 Timothy 2:22

In other words: Recognize you're potential to sin; Avoid influences that could influence youthful lusts; Pursue, Faith, love and peace; Spend time with other believers whose hearts are pure.

Spiritual warfare:

Be self-controlled and alert. Your enemy the devil prowls around like a roaring lion looking for someone to devour. Resist him, standing firm in the faith, because you know that your brothers throughout the world are undergoing the same kind of sufferings.–1 Peter 5:8

One of the things I learned in the spiritual warfare I have been facing throughout the years is that the Devil does not fight fair. He does not attack you where you are strong, but where you are the most vulnerable. He likes to exhaust you, trample you, and do whatever he can do to get you separated from the protective wings of God.

Some of the areas of spiritual warfare we can be confronted with are in the area of pride, fear, control and rejection. Just focusing on rejection, we learn very quickly that he uses people to make us feel rejected. Especially during times, and from people that you would least expect it from; from those who you thought were with you and for you; or from people you trusted to be fighting the same battle.

It is at those times you can find yourself becoming angry, sarcastic, critical and bitter. You would want to fight back, and hurt those who have hurt you. Or you would like to run away and hide. But God, through the power of the Holy Spirit keeps reminding us that "*Our struggle is not against flesh and blood, but against the rulers, against the authorities, against the powers of this dark world and against the spiritual forces of evil in the heavenly realms. Therefore put on the full armor of God, so that when the day of evil comes, you may be able to stand your ground*"–Ephesians 6:12-13

For me it is a reminder that I am in warfare against an enemy who will do anything he can to destroy me, the relationships we are having with our brothers and sisters in the Lord, and most of all, our relationship with God. It means that I need to protect that relationship, by spending time with Him, being prayed up, and continuing to forgive those who—often without even knowing—have hurt me, so that nothing will hinder my relationship with Jesus.

We have His help to overcome

Everyone has heard about your obedience, so I am full of joy over you; but I want you to be wise about what is good, and innocent about what is evil. The God of peace will soon crush Satan under your feet. The grace of our Lord Jesus be with you.–Romans 16:19-20

It is not easy to live pure and holy lives in the midst of the sinful and corrupt world we live in. We live with the temptation to compromise and the continual chance for falling into sin. *("The spirit is willing, but the body is weak."– Mark 14:38).* But there is also a reason for not falling. One of the great statements of the Bible is this: *"No temptation has seized you except what is common to man. And God is faithful; he will not let you be tempted beyond what you can bear. But when you are tempted, He will also provide a way out so that you can stand up under it"–1 Corinthians 10:13.*

Humans all experience similar temptations. But God is faithful and provides for all of us the power to say no or to take action that enables us to lead a life of purity.

Paul advised Titus:
'For the grace of God that brings salvation has appeared to all men. It teaches us to say "No" to ungodliness and worldly passions, and to live self-controlled, upright, and godly lives in this present age, while we wait for the blessed hope, the glorious appearing of our great God and Savior, Jesus Christ, who gave himself for us to redeem us from all wickedness and to purify for himself a people that are his very own, eager to do what is good.'–Titus 2:11-14

The Bible clearly tells us that when we receive Jesus Christ as Savior and Lord, the Holy Spirit enters our life and makes our body his temple. The Holy Spirit living in us causes us a new sensitivity to sin. Every time we are tempted, the Spirit of God is right there to give us strength to overcome that temptation. We can live in victory when we trust the enabling grace of God to keep us from practicing sin.

The choice is ours.

"For if you live according to the sinful nature, you will die; but if by the Spirit you put to death the misdeeds of the body, you will live, because those who are led by the Spirit of God are sons of God"–Romans 8:13-14.

Victory depends on the direction in which we yield. If we yield to the old nature, we fall into sin; if we yield to the Spirit, we have victory. So when we are faced with decisions, when we are at a crossroads in temptation, when we are tempted to do things our own way, we need to pray over it, and seek the guidance of the Spirit of God in our life to help us make the decision that leads to victory. And then…make the choice to obey!

3. Being Teachable

"Come to me, all you who are weary and burdened, and I will give you rest. Take my yoke upon you and learn from me, for I am gentle and humble in heart, and you will find rest for your souls. For my yoke is easy and my burden is light."–Matthew 11:28-30

The first two decades of my life I learned a lot of things both good and bad. And yes, many things I learned I had to learn the hard way. There were things that would stifle my spiritual growth, unless I would un-learn them. Have you ever noticed certain qualities of your parents that you detest? You see a trait or a quirk and proudly swear you'll never do that. You'll never be like them, but then years later you look back and realize that in many ways you are just like them? Good and bad qualities alike? Sadly enough, I know by looking back that I picked up some of them as well.

I learned that I needed to change in the area of:

My behavior.

In my life I was taught to deal with life's challenges and pressures the world's way. It is amazing how much bad behavior you can pick up from your environment. You remember what I said about my stepfather's philosophy, that it did not matter how he did things, as long as he obtained the result he desired. How did I hate that—But "O boy," what would I copy when I was not careful!

My choices.

I had to stand on my own two feet, and take responsibility for my life, without depending on others, and blaming them when things went wrong. I did not want to repeat the same mistakes I had made before, or model myself after the wrong choices I had seen other people make.

My Beliefs.

Yes, I went to church the first fifteen years of my life. I went to Sunday school, and church. I had learned a lot from the preachers and teachers I had listened too, however it was still their opinions, and I had never discovered these things for myself. And when I seriously wanted to grow spiritually, and continue ministering to other people, I knew I needed to learn what the Bible had to teach me. For the truth is, "You can't give what you don't have."

Jesus said, *"Take my yoke upon you and learn from me…"* In other words, "Be my Disciple."

The Biblical word, "Disciples," is translated from the Greek word Mathetes (Strong's exhaustive concordance of the Bible #1301) which means also a learner or pupil. When you look up the word "disciple" in the Webster dictionary, you find that its basic meaning is "a follower of." For example we could compare it with apprenticeship of a trade such as an electrician. The younger less experienced electrician (the disciple) gets trained, or is mentored by the older, more experienced electrician.

During the time Jesus lived, in the culture around Him, the disciple was expected to live with his teacher and to share his experiences as well as to hear his teachings.

The disciple was also expected to "abide" in his teacher's words, which we can read in John 8:31, where Jesus said to the believers: *"If you abide in My Word, you are my disciples indeed."* This means that the disciples needed to take on the teacher's words as the pattern for their own way of life, putting all that the teacher taught into daily practice.

The goal of the discipleship was not just gaining and sharing head knowledge, but the disciple was expected to become like his teacher in word and deed.

Jesus spoke in Luke 6:40 *"A disciple is not above his teacher, but everyone who is perfectly trained will be like his teacher."* This form of discipleship was designed to shape the character of the learner, as well as his thinking. Jesus introduced an added dimension and goal of discipleship in the lives of those who were learning of him. When fully discipled, his followers were to be like him, despite their diverse and at times irreconcilable individuality.

The disciple in Christianity is a follower of Jesus Christ, desiring to discover his ways and apply them to his life. This means that a disciple has to be open and teachable. He is a follower who desires to learn. Being a learner involves perceiving concepts, building life principles, and acquiring knowledge. We find skills subsequently in the application of what we've learned through activities such as evangelism, leading a Bible study, or teaching a Sunday school class. The apostle Paul told the Philippians to put into practice what they had learned from him through observation (see Philippians 4:9). Paul not only communicated with what he taught, but he was a model to the Philippians in what he did. Paul reminded another church:

"You became imitators of us and of the Lord; in spite of severe suffering, you welcomed the message with the joy given by the Holy Spirit. And so you became a model to all the believers in Macedonia and Achaia"–1 Thessalonians 1:6-7. They imitated the model they had been given, the Apostle Paul, and in turn became models to other believers in the two provinces.

We have to be sure that the model we follow is Jesus Christ, even as Paul did. "Follow my example, as I follow the example of Christ"–1 Corinthians 11:1. The Christian disciple must be both a learner of biblical truth and a visible follower of Jesus Christ. This unbeatable combination makes a tremendous impact on others.

Areas of spiritual growth:

Focusing on spiritual growth, I believe that there are five qualities we need to pay attention to.

Our character.

With a genuine Christ-honoring character we are to produce other men and women who will represent Christ to the world the same way we are.

If a follower of Jesus is functioning as he should, Jesus said that men would recognize them as his disciples (see John 13:35). The Bible says that as disciples we are to reflect like mirrors the glory of the Lord. Paul wrote,

"And we, who with unveiled faces all reflect the Lord's glory, are being transformed into his likeness with ever-increasing glory, which comes from the Lord, who is the Spirit."–2 Corinthians 3:18

In a Christian, character qualities are basically those Christ like qualities that are the fruit of the Holy Spirit living in us. These include: love, joy, peace, patience, kindness, goodness, faithfulness, gentleness and self-control (Galatians 5:22-23). These qualities are what people will remember us by. People should see our love, our joy in the Lord, our peace—the fact that nothing seems to destroy the tranquility of our vital relationship with Christ; our longsuffering when we bear the pressures of life as God would have us. When we demonstrate kindness and goodness toward others as we would the Lord, then our inner character stands out for all to see. People should see our faith, which is our confidence in God's trustworthiness and promises; our meekness, which is our recognition that God alone is our defense and capable of handling any mistreatment by others; and our self-control.

Paul wrote to Timothy: *"In a large house there are articles not only of gold and silver, but also of wood and clay; some are for noble purposes and some for ignoble. If a man cleanses himself from the latter, he will be an instrument for noble purposes, made holy, useful to the Master and prepared to do any good work."–2 Timothy 2:20-21.*

The Apostle Paul Reminds us: *"Do you not know that your body is a temple of the Holy Spirit, who is in you, whom you have received from God? You are not your own; you were bought at a price. Therefore honor God with your body"* (i.e. your lifestyle).–1 Corinthians 6:19-20

The disciple as a learner and follower must have a commitment to develop his character so it will reflect Jesus Christ.

A walk of grace and mercy

Jesus said: "Do you see this woman? I came into your house. You did

not give me any water for my feet, but she wet my feet with her tears and wiped them with her hair. You did not give me a kiss, but this woman, from the time I entered, has not stopped kissing my feet. You did not put oil on my head, but she has poured perfume on my feet. Therefore, I tell you, her many sins have been forgiven—for she loved much. But he who has been forgiven little loves little." Then Jesus said to her, "Your sins are forgiven."–Luke 7: 44-48

In the story we learn about gratefulness in action. Look at the words of Jesus: *"she loved much. But he who has been forgiven little loves little."* God does not just want us to become benefactors of His blessings, He want us to respond to our environment with the same graces as he has bestowed them on us. As Jesus has blessed us, He gave us an example how we too should bless others. Let's remember we really did not deserve His grace. The same can be said about the area of forgiveness.

Jesus teaching us to pray said: *"...For if you forgive men when they sin against you, your heavenly Father will also forgive you. But if you do not forgive men their sins, your Father will not forgive your sins."*–Matthew 6:14-15

Loving and forgiving is our choice to make

Out of my own personal experience I know that there are times that loving and forgiving can be about impossible. We do not feel we have the smallest grain of strength in our system left to be merciful to those who wronged us and hurt us; especially when they have repeated their offense. However we need to remember that the extension of grace ought not to be based on our feelings, but ought to be our choice. We need to ask our self, "Is Jesus worth it"? Or, "Do I love Jesus enough to be merciful to those who have hurt me?" When you feel this way, go to God and tell Him about the feelings of hurt, anger, or frustration you might feel at those times. And when you struggle in the area of loving and forgiving, think about the words of Jesus, while he was hanging on the cross. After He was falsely accused, abused, ridiculed and forsaken. He said, *"Father, forgive them, for they do not know what they are doing."*–Luke 23:34

I remember the condition of the relationship I had with my stepfather. It was a very difficult and dysfunctional one. It seemed that when anything went bad, I was the first to blame. It made me resentful of him to the point I started to think and daydream of being older and bigger, and about all the ways I could hurt him back. It was after my salvation experience, during one of my devotions that God started to expose my anger and resentment towards my stepfather. God asked me to forgive him. My response to God was,

"I can't forgive him. Lord, don't you know what he has done to me? There's no way!"

But God kept patiently repeating Himself to me. He said, "When you love me, forgive him." Finally in answer I remember telling God,

"There's nothing in me to forgive him with. It doesn't exist…yet because I love you Lord I will make the choice to forgive my stepfather. But, you'd better change the feelings I have towards him, because I can not change them myself."

Believe it or not, it was a couple of months later that I was forced to face my stepfather at the mall. First I tried to escape the encounter hoping desperately that he had not seen me. I really did not want to confront the man or my feelings. But when I noticed he had seen me, I started to walk towards him with the most intense turmoil of emotions passing through my mind. While I was still thinking about how to hurt him, to my great surprise, when I caught up to him, the only thing I could say were the words, "Hi, how are you"? I could not believe that I had said that. It was at that time that I learned that even though my memory of the hurt was still there, the pain that had accompanied it for all those years was gone. After my choice to forgive my stepfather, not only did God perform a miracle in me, but He also gave me that grace I lacked to extend toward my stepfather.

When you find your self struggling in this area, pray something like this: Father, I do not feel like it, but I want to make the choice to love, and the choice to forgive. However I can not do it in my own strength. My memories are hurting too much. Please take away the pain and change that what I can not change in myself. Let the circumstances of my life and relationships change for the better. In Jesus name–Amen.

Faithfulness in ministry.

Throughout the years we have learned that the quality of a person's character will be reflected in his or her ministry. If a person is mature in character, he will have an effective ministry; if he is immature or there are weaknesses in his character, he will not have much of a ministry. Faithfulness leads to proficiency just as commitment is the key to excellence. These were important characteristics in the ministry of the Lord Jesus. *"People were overwhelmed with amazement. 'He has done everything well,' they said"*–Mark 7:37.

As a follower of Jesus Christ, we must try to do everything well. Each one of us who would be Christ's disciple must strive for the development of the ministry skills with which God has equipped him. We need to be faithful in our use of the spiritual gifts God has given and carry out our responsibility well. If we concentrate on the quality of our life and witness, quantity will come with time and faithfulness; there will be great fruitfulness.

"Whoever can be trusted with very little can also be trusted with much, and whoever is dishonest with very little will also be dishonest with much.–Luke 16:10

Paul says an interesting thing in his letter to the Corinthians:

"Now when I went to Troas to preach the gospel of Christ and found that the Lord had opened a door for me, I still had no peace of mind, because I did not find my brother Titus there. So I said good-by to them and went on to Macedonia"–2 Corinthians 2:12-13. Paul left a promising ministry to go and look for Titus. Why would he give up the opportunity to reach a whole city for Christ to go search for one man? Because: *Titus was more important to Paul than Troas*. Paul knew very well that with proper training Titus would become proficient in the ministry and multiply believers many times over. Paul could reach many more cities with the gospel than just Troas if he had the right man.

And Titus was the right man, for quality is more important then quantity. Quality should be visible in every area of our ministry. When we realize that whatever we are presently doing is for Jesus Christ, then we will be more concerned about quality that is visible to others.

Appearance is one other aspect of our ministry that should not be overlooked. I am not telling you that we have to wear a suit and tie, but we can be clean and look approachable.

Remember, we are representing Him, The King of King's! If we want to exalt Jesus Christ, we must be willing to pay the price for quality. The cost may be high, but the results are tremendous.

Whatever you do, work at it with all your heart, as working for the Lord, not for men, since you know that you will receive an inheritance from the Lord as a reward. It is the Lord Christ you are serving.– Colossians 3:23-24

A disciple must develop convictions that are their own

And without faith it is impossible to please God, because anyone who comes to him must believe that he exists and that he rewards those who earnestly seek him.–Hebrews 11:6

There comes a time in our life when it is no longer valid for us to base what we believe on the convictions of others—like our parents, pastors, or perhaps other people we look up too. We must develop convictions that are our own. We find an excellent example of that in the life of Moses. *"By faith Moses, when he had grown up, refused to be known as the son of Pharaoh's daughter. He chose to be mistreated along with the people of God rather than to enjoy the pleasures of sin for a short time"–Hebrews 11:24-25.* Moses came to the place where the convictions he had learned from his parents had to become his own or had to be abandoned.

Personal convictions for the Christian are very important. A Christian must stand out as being different from the world. But convictions are also vital in the more spiritual aspects of our life. If we have convictions about being disciples and making disciples, then we will both be and make disciples. The reality is that when a person has convictions, he will make important decisions based on them, but if he does not have convictions, he won't use the methods. It is kind of the way we translate the law, when we have conservative views and convictions we will translate the law from that position, when we have liberal views and convictions we will translate the law from those standards. Or, to give you another example, let's talk about watching TV. When we have strong convictions about the things we ought to watch and not to watch, we will make sure we will only look at things which are acceptable to us. On the other hand, when you do not share in those strong convictions, you will watch what ever it is you feel like watching.

Reading the Gospels, Jesus Christ did not give us many details about how the Great Commission was to be carried out. He simply told us to do it. Because he told us to do it, we should have strong convictions about its importance and look for ways to do so.

Looking ahead

All these people were still living by faith when they died. They did not receive the things promised; they only saw them and welcomed them from a distance. And they admitted that they were aliens and strangers on earth.–Hebrews 11:13

Some people have the ability to see what is directly in front of you as well as what is down the road in the distance. We have often the problem of only seeing the now, the immediate. We have a hard time seeing what the long-range results of our actions might be. It is imperative that we ask ourselves daily whether we are doing anything of merit that will pay off in the future. Looking ahead might cause one to pray something like this: "Lord, if you let me live in this community, allow me to leave behind some people who have had an encounter with Christ and been discipled because of my lifestyle."

Looking ahead includes a positive view of our immediate circumstances.

Let me ask you, how do you view your circumstances? Can you see them as hindrances or as stepping stones? Can they be viewed as defeats or as wonderful opportunities?

The person who has right perspective will view all the circumstances of life as stepping stones to better things and choose to act upon them in faith as the great opportunities of life, which God has given. Consequently, the believer should always be looking down the road, not seeing just the present but the future as well.

Do not be deceived: God cannot be mocked. A man reaps what he sows. The one who sows to please his sinful nature, from that nature will reap destruction; the one who sows to please the Spirit, from the Spirit will reap eternal life. Let us not become weary in doing good, for at the proper time we will reap a harvest if we do not give up. Therefore, as we have opportunity, let us do good to all people, especially to those who belong to the family of believers.–Galatians 6:7-10

How do we build conviction and perspective into our life?

Three guidelines apply equally to our own life as well as the lives of others:

Focus on principles rather than methods.

Don't just copy what everybody else is doing without discerning what God has to say about it.

We need to remember that every person, every culture, and every circumstance is unique, and mite needs a different approach.

The person who is more concerned about methods of evangelism or follow-up, rather than the necessity of evangelism or follow-up will often never be involved in either one. The person with conviction and perspective uses whatever methods are available to him and gets the job done. Since principles are universal, they will work anywhere, at any time. But strategies may have to vary from place to place, time to time, or from culture to culture. We need to focus on the "why" of what we are doing, emphasizing the purpose rather than the skills.

It is the purpose that will develop the skills. When we know why we are doing something, then it is easier to do what we are supposed to do. It is certainly important to learn the skill of evangelism, but unless we know why we should be evangelizing, the skill may remain unused.

Concentrate on trusting God rather than learning man's theories about him.

I keep asking that the God of our Lord Jesus Christ, the glorious Father, may give you the Spirit of wisdom and revelation, so that you may know him better.–Ephesians 1:17

A disciple has to learn to place their trust in God. This means walking by faith. It is this firm trust in God that will help us develop convictions and perspective.

Some people have theories about God and walking by faith, but they need to experience it practically. We may not become giants of faith immediately, but neither did the people described in the Bible. We learn to walk by faith just like a child learns to walk physically. The Christian disciple begins with the first step of faith. Then he may fall, but he tries again. And as he persists in trusting God, he learns how to walk by faith.

Jesus Christ said, *"But seek first his kingdom and his righteousness, and all these things will be given to you as well"–Matthew 6:33.*

The Lord is saying that we are to concentrate on trusting God and he will provide. This is the major principle of living by faith.

I love the words of the Apostle Paul found in Philippians 4:4-9; *"Rejoice in the Lord always. I will say it again: Rejoice! Let your gentleness be evident to all. The Lord is near!* (He makes a great expression of faith). Do not be anxious about anything, but in everything, by prayer and petition, with thanksgiving, present your requests to God. And the peace of God, which transcends all understanding, will guard your hearts and your minds in Christ Jesus. Finally, brothers, whatever is true, whatever is noble, whatever is right, whatever is pure, whatever is lovely, whatever is admirable—if anything is excellent or praiseworthy—think about such things. Whatever you have learned or received or heard from me, or seen in me—put it into practice. And the God of peace will be with you."

Complete what you started; be committed to finish the task; and don't give up.

Therefore, my dear brothers, stand firm. Let nothing move you. Always give yourselves fully to the work of the Lord, because you know that your labor in the Lord is not in vain.–1 Corinthians 15:58

Involved in this is a high view of God and his ability to provide for all of our needs. This is what Scripture says of Abraham: *"He did not waver through unbelief regarding the promise of God, but was strengthened in his faith and gave glory to God, being fully persuaded that God had power to do what he had promised"–Romans 4:20-21.*

A disciple, then, is a follower and a learner committed to developing his character and growing more Christ like. When we are willing to learn, we emerge as trophies of his grace and products of his tender, loving care.

Jesus, God's Living Word

Jesus said: "I am the way and the truth and the life. No one comes to the Father except through me.–John 14:6

A disciple demonstrates faithfulness and a desire to learn about Jesus. He has the desire to know Him, and Understand Him. He desires to know and apply the word of God through hearing it preached, and taught. His motivation is to make Gods Word His highest form of authority. The Bible is the means by which God has revealed himself to mankind. In it are all the things we need to know for faith and practice. It is God's final word to man about living in this world and knowing that we have eternal life.

The Bible Reveals the God of Salvation to Us

Just as Moses lifted up the snake in the desert, so the Son of Man must be lifted up, that everyone who believes in him may have eternal life. "For God so loved the world that he gave his one and only Son, that whoever believes in him shall not perish but have eternal life. For God did not send his Son into the world to condemn the world, but to save the world through him.–John 3:14-17

James tells us that God "chose to give us birth through the word of truth, that we might be a kind of first fruits of all he created" (James 1:18). Peter wrote, *"For you have been born again, not of perishable seed, but of imperishable, through the living and enduring word of God" 1 Peter 1:23.* It is through the word of God that we recognize and acknowledge our need of a Savior from sin. The Holy Spirit uses the Scriptures to reveal the needs of people.

The Bible tells us that everything that has been written in it was *"to teach us, so that through endurance and the encouragement of the Scriptures we might have hope"–Romans 15:4.* The biblical concept of hope has in it the sense of certainty, of knowing that we have eternal life with God.

The psalmist wrote, *"Salvation is far from the wicked, for they do not seek out your decrees"–Psalm 119:155.* What the psalmist is saying is that no one will be saved apart from the word of God. The wicked do not find salvation because they will not consider the Scriptures, which are used by the Holy Spirit to pierce our heart and bring us to God through Jesus Christ.

The Bible reveals us of our sinfulness

For the word of God is living and active. Sharper than any double-edged sword, it penetrates even to dividing soul and spirit, joints and marrow; it judges the thoughts and attitudes of the heart.–Hebrews 4:12;

In order to lead a pure life, the disciple must be sensitive to sin. The only way we can be sensitive to sin is to be teachable, pliable and correctable to the work of the Holy Spirit, and by reading the word of God, which enables us to recognize our sins. We confess our sin to God, and so are cleansed from them. No one can ever sit down with his Bible, read it carefully, and not experience the ministry of the Holy Spirit dealing with him about certain sins in his life.

The psalmist once asked, "How can a young man keep his way pure?" And he quickly answered: *"By living according to your word. I seek you with all my heart; do not let me stray from your commands. I have hidden your word in my heart that I might not sin against you" Psalm 119:9-11.* Note that it says *"might not sin against you,"* not, "cannot." We can still sin if we choose to. We have to allow God's word to convict us so we would obey it.

When you are having problems with undesirable habits, the answer is to get into the word of God. Regular Bible study, Scripture memory, and application of God's word to your life will do wonders for you. A regular diet of the word of God enables the Holy Spirit to use the Scriptures to deal with our sins and changes us where we need to change.

The Christian disciple must grow spiritually.

If he does not grow spiritually, he is stagnating and stops being a disciple. Our spiritual growth is directly dependent on our spiritual diet of the word of God as our spiritual food.

The writer to the Hebrews divides biblical intake into milk and meat. *"In fact, though by this time you ought to be teachers, you need someone to teach you the elementary truths of God's word all over again. You need milk, not solid food!"–Hebrews 5:12.*

New converts need the milk of the word so that they can begin to grow through that intake of spiritual nourishment (see 1 Peter 2:2-3). However we should not remain stuck in the basic "A, B, C's" of Christianity. The disciple, ought to be taking in "solid food" or "meat" for growth beyond the "newborn" stage. Milk will help us grow to a certain point (just like physical children), but after that we will need meat for continued spiritual growth. We are built up and progress in our sanctification by the word of God. It is an important principle in our spiritual growth, for we have the capacity to continue growing spiritually throughout our Christian life.

When Paul addressed the elders of the church at Ephesus, he was speaking to a group of men who were certainly disciples. He challenged them with these words: *"Now I commit you to God and to the word of his grace, which can build you up and give you an inheritance among all those who are sanctified"–Acts 20:32.*

The Bible brings guidance for our life

"Your word is a lamp to my feet and a light for my path."–Psalm 119:105

King Solomon wrote:

Trust in the LORD with all your heart and lean not on your own understanding; in all your ways acknowledge him, and he will make your paths straight.–Proverbs 3:5, 6

The disciple looks to the word of God for guidance concerning the will of God for his life. God has promised to lead us, but in order to know what God has for us; we must be in his word.

If we trust God concerning the direction of our life, he promises to give us some of our innermost desires that are according to his will. The psalmist wrote: *"Delight yourself in the Lord and he will give you the desires of your heart. Commit your way to the Lord; trust in him and he will do this"– Psalm 37:4-5.*

The Bible Empowers Us in Our message to the World

God was reconciling the world to himself in Christ, not counting men's sins against them. And he has committed to us the message of reconciliation. We are therefore Christ's ambassadors, as though God were making his appeal through us. We implore you on Christ's behalf: Be reconciled to God–2 Corinthians 5:19-20.

Another reason the disciple is to be in the word of God is so that he might witness effectively for Christ. We can never be fruitful in leading people to the Savior unless we know the Scriptures. We have to have something to say to unbelievers. God told Ezekiel: *"The people to whom I am sending you are obstinate and stubborn. Say to them, 'This is what the Sovereign Lord says"–Ezekiel 2:4.* That's what God specifically commissioned Paul to do. "Then he (Ananias) said: *'The God of our fathers has chosen you to know his will and to see the Righteous One and to hear words from his mouth. You will be his witness to all men of what you have seen and heard"–Acts 22:14-15.*

Our message when we witness should be, "This is what God says!" An ambassador does not say what he wants to say, but only what he is told to say.

A great passage on the necessity of the word of God for a strong witness is found in Solomon's Proverbs. God speaking through the writer said, *"Have I not written thirty sayings for you, sayings of counsel and knowledge, teaching you true and reliable words, so that you can give sound answers to him who sent you?"–Proverbs 22:20-21.*

Paul stated, *"All Scripture is God-breathed and is useful for teaching, rebuking, correcting and training in righteousness, so that the man of God may be thoroughly equipped for every good work"–2 Timothy 3:16-17.* Everything in our Christian life, our character, our words, our actions, our experiences is related to biblical teaching or "doctrine." The Scripture is what we believe in and what we do; it is the basis of our faith, its very foundation. People may have false concepts or wrong premises, but they are basing their lives on the teaching they have received. You can tell quite a bit about a person's doctrine or convictions by the manner of that person's life.

A disciple needs to know which pad to follow.

"Enter through the narrow gate. For wide is the gate and broad is the road that leads to destruction, and many enter through it. But small is the gate and narrow the road that leads to life and only a few find it.– Matthew 7:13.14;

The Bible serves as a mirror to show us exactly what we are like. The Bible not only tells us when and were we have sinned, but it also provides the corrective steps necessary for the restoration of fellowship with God and with our fellowmen.

The Bible tells us how to live a life pleasing to God, how to live harmoniously with our fellowmen, both Christians and non-Christians, and how to live in this world under the domination of the evil one. For all of us there are times that we get off the "straight and narrow" path. At first we may not notice it because we are still so close to the right track, but after a while it deviates further. Most sins do not show themselves as a sudden, abrupt change, and so sometimes are hard to recognize. But after a certain time, when we have strayed some distance from the right path, the Holy Spirit rebukes us through God's word and we are faced with a choice. We can disregard him and keep going farther and farther away from God's ways. Or we can take steps of corrective action and return to the word of God for further training in righteousness.

Knowing God's Word helps us to understand God.

This is what the LORD says: "Let not the wise man boast of his wisdom or the strong man boast of his strength or the rich man boast of his riches, but let him who boasts boast about this: that he understands and knows me, that I am the LORD, who exercises kindness, justice and righteousness on earth, for in these I delight," declares the LORD.– Jeremiah 9:23, 24

God's word teaches us that we can get into the Scriptures in a number of ways. We hear the word of God, we read it, we study it, we memorize it, and we meditate on what we have heard, read, studied, and memorized.

Hearing the Word of God

"Consequently, faith comes from hearing the message, and the message is heard through the word of Christ"–Romans 10:17.

Our first responsibility is to hear the word of God regularly from godly teachers. When you hear the word preached, a servant of God is communicating the Lord's message to you. We can hear the word of God at our worship services, in Sunday school or at a Bible school. We can hear it on the radio and television. We can hear it at conferences, seminars, and on CD's, DVD's or tapes. To help you remember what you have heard, make it a practice to take notes. You see, a disciple is not merely a hearer of the word of God, but he is a doer of it.

Do not merely listen to the word, and so deceive yourselves. Do what it says. Anyone who listens to the word but does not do what it says is like a man who looks at his face in a mirror and, after looking at himself, goes away and immediately forgets what he looks like. But the man who looks intently into the perfect law that gives freedom, and continues to do this, not forgetting what he has heard, but doing it, he will be blessed in what he does–James 1:22-25.

Reading the Word of God

In ancient Israel the king was required to read the word of God "all the days of his life so that he may learn to revere the Lord his God and follow carefully all the words of this law and these decrees" (Deuteronomy 17:19). John promised blessings for those who would read God's word (see Revelation 1:3), and Paul urged Timothy to devote himself to the public reading of the Scriptures (see 1 Timothy 4:13). Christian disciples should be reading the word of God regularly.

Studying the Word of God

My son, if you accept my words and store up my commands within you, turning your ear to wisdom and applying your heart to understanding, and if you call out for insight and cry aloud for understanding, and if you look for it as for silver and search for it as for hidden treasure, then you will understand the fear of the LORD and find the knowledge of God.– Proverbs 2:1-4

One other means of intake of the word of God is study or careful investigation of the Scriptures. King Solomon urged us to search for wisdom as though we were looking for silver and treasure (Proverbs 2:4). The Bible is the source of all wisdom. Paul told Timothy to *"do your best to present yourself to God as one approved, a workman who does not need to be ashamed and who correctly handles the word of truth"–2 Timothy 2:15.* The Bible commends the "noble" Bereans because they "examined the Scriptures every day" to see if Paul was telling them the truth from God (Acts 17:11). So both by precept and example, Bible study is taught as a necessity in the life of a disciple. Let your Bible study be consistent, systematic, original, practical and investigative

Study the Bible, not only books about the Bible. It is helpful to use concordances, and commentaries. Also a question-and-answer Bible study could provide opportunities to make discoveries and help you draw some new conclusions.

Ask yourself questions like:

What does the passage say? In your own words summarize or outline the passage under study. Do not try to interpret, but try to reproduce the thoughts of the writer in your own words.

What does the passage say that I do not understand? In this step list the problems that you have with the passage verse by verse. This does not necessarily mean that you will find answers for every problem, but it is recognition that there are some things here which you do not understand.

What do other passages of Scripture say that help me understand this passage? This exercise is often called finding cross-references, other Scriptures that say the same thing, or in some way help explain the verse in the passage under study. This is usually done with the help of a concordance.

Do word studies, using Hebrew and Greek dictionaries.

Do not be afraid to read different commentaries to compare their thoughts with yours.

Write out how you will put into practice the teaching of the application verse or passage. Set a date to check up on yourself to make sure you have carried out what you planned.

Remember: The benefits of Bible study are not something that we keep for our self, but we use them in our ministry to help others.

Memorizing the Word of God

"Let the word of Christ dwell in you richly as you teach and admonish one another with all wisdom"–Colossians 3:16.

The Scriptures are full of passages that indicate that God wants us to saturate our life with his word. Both the Old and New Testaments emphasize a relationship to God's word that can only come from Scripture memory. *"These commandments that I give you today are to be upon your hearts"– Deuteronomy 6:6. "Keep my commands and you will live; guard my teachings as the apple of your eye. Bind them on your fingers; write them on the tablet of your heart"–Proverbs 7:2-3.* Since Scripture indicates without question that we are to memorize the word of God, we have only the options of obedience and disobedience.

Some advantages of memorizing the word of God:

It increases our knowledge of the word of God, and our faith and trust in

God. We begin to look at life more and more from his point of view. Paul wrote, *"Your attitude should be the same as that of Christ Jesus"–Philippians 2:5*. The memorized word of God enables us to have the mind of Christ at all times as we walk through life and thus builds our faith in his guidance and leading.

It helps us to obey Him and have victory over sin. The psalmist wrote, *"I have hidden your word in my heart that I might not sin against you"–Psalm 119:11*.

"Whoever has my commands and obeys them, he is the one who loves me. He who loves me will be loved by my Father, and I too will love him and show myself to him."–John 14:21 Knowing this verse enables us to turn to the passage to get further teaching on obeying the commands of God.

Enables Christian growth. Peter wrote about this to new Christians. *"Like newborn babies, crave pure spiritual milk, so that by it you may grow up in your salvation"–1 Peter 2:2*. The same craving or desire should continue to be true as we mature in our faith.

Gives guidance. The psalmist has recorded God saying, *"I will instruct you and teach you in the way you should go; I will counsel you and watch over you"–Psalm 32:8*. One way God does that today is through his word.

Improves our prayer life. Jesus tells us, *"If you remain in me and my words remain in you, ask whatever you wish, and it will be given you"–John 15:7*. It enhances our prayer life if we pray Scripture back to God. Memorizing key verses on prayer encourages us to pray and helps us remember how to pray. Jesus said, *"Until now you have not asked for anything in my name. Ask and you will receive, and your joy will be complete"–John 16:24*.

John wrote: *"This is the assurance we have in approaching God: that if we ask anything according to his will, he hears us. And if we know that he hears us, whatever we ask, we know that we have what we asked of him"–1 John 5:14-15*.

It leads us in a spirit of worship. In our private worship we are able to praise God through memorized praise passages of the Psalms (Examples: Psalms 8, 9, 100, 117, 145-150).

It helps us to become the right example for others to follow. Christians and non-Christians alike are always challenged by someone who knows the word of God. They realize that he has taken the time to memorize it and retain it. Challenge others with your example as Paul challenged others with these words: *"Whatever you have learned or received or heard from me, or seen in me, put it into practice"–Philippians 4:9.*
. When people who ask us about our faith. Peter, in his first letter to Christ's followers, said *"be prepared to give an answer to everyone who asks you to give the reason for the hope that you have"–1 Peter 3:15.* We may not have the printed word of God available, but we are never without the memorized word. The Prophet Isaiah wrote, *"The Sovereign Lord has given me an instructed tongue, to know the word that sustains the weary"– Isaiah 50:4.* The Holy Spirit will remind us of the needed verses for each individual.

To give you a suggestion for scripture memorization: Start early in the week and day to learn a new verse. Ask the Holy Spirit to help you; Write it down; Carry your verses with you; Read it again when you have the opportunity; Use what you are memorizing in your personal ministry.

Meditating on the Word of God

Blessed is the man who does not walk in the counsel of the wicked or stand in the way of sinners or sit in the seat of mockers. But his delight is in the law of the Lord, and on his law he meditates day and night. He is like a tree planted by streams of water, which yields its fruit in season and whose leaf does not wither. Whatever he does prospers–Psalm 1:1-3.

This Psalm states that the person who will meditate on God's word will be blessed, prosperous, and successful. The man or woman who wants to be a disciple of the Lord Jesus Christ must commit himself wholly to every means of intake of the word of God on a regular basis: hearing, reading, studying, memorizing, and meditating on it.

4. Filled with the Holy Spirit

On one occasion, while he was eating with them, he gave them this command: "Do not leave Jerusalem, but wait for the gift my Father promised, which you have heard me speak about. For John baptized with water, but in a few days you will be baptized with the Holy Spirit."–Acts 1:4-5

My salvation experience led me into the Baptism of the Holy Spirit. Please understand I did not know anything about the Holy Spirit at that time. The church denomination which I had come out of had never really done any teaching about Him. Commonly, our leaders held that the belief that after the last Apostle died, it this was the end of the Baptism of the Holy Spirit, and all that was related to it.

Being afraid of what might happen with me on that ship, and desperate for a miracle, I reached out to that little Bible I had received before I left to be a sailor. It was not that I knew what to look for, but I was reaching out to the last straw of hope I had before I would go to the deep. While I was holding the Bible in my hand, and praying for mercy, several Biblical stories went through my mind. It was not that I remembered the places were they were found. But one of the verses that went trough my mind was, that God was the same yesterday, today and forever. Following this verse thoughts about Moses flooded my mind, and how God spoke to him out of a burning bush. How God fed His people with bread and meat in the desert, how He caused water to flow out of a rock, and how He split the waters so that His people could cross the Red sea. (Exodus 3–14) I started to wonder to myself, "Why did the pastor never put the verse and the stories about Moses together? Why did he never talk about stuff like that? When it is true that God would be "the same yesterday, today and forever," then God would still be able to do what he did many years ago. Meaning, God would still occasionally speak to people, he would still meet the needs of the people, and he would still help people out of trouble. So I started to pray, "God, when you are still the same today as you were in the time of Moses, I need you to help me, I need you to speak to me, I need you to show me what to do."

Opening my Bible, still uncertain what to look for, the pages fell to John 14:15-18. The way the verses caught my eye, it was as if that part was highlighted. It was were Jesus said, *"If ye love me, keep my commandments. And I will pray the Father, and he shall give you another Comforter, that he may abide with you for ever; Even the Spirit of truth; whom the world cannot receive, because it sees him not, neither knows him: but you know him; for he dwells with you, and shall be in you. I will not leave you comfortless: I will come to you."* Not quite knowing what this verse meant, I knew one thing for certain: I needed comfort and had felt like an orphan for many years. Yet here, Jesus said that when I was going to obey, he was going to send a comforter to me. Not knowing who that would be—perhaps a friend or a girlfriend, I said "yes God send me that comforter you are talking about in this scripture." And then, still not being sure if God was speaking to me, or that He really meant this promise, I opened to another page of the Bible. And again, it was like that part was highlighted too, it said: *"So I say to you: Ask and it will be given to you; seek and you will find; knock and the door will be opened to you. For everyone who asks receives; he who seeks finds; and to him who knocks, the door will be opened. "Which of you fathers, if your son asks for a fish, will give him a snake instead? Or if he asks for an egg, will give him a scorpion? If you then, though you are evil, know how to give good gifts to your children, how much more will your Father in heaven give the Holy Spirit to those who ask him!"–Luke 11:9-13*

The words, "If you then, though you are evil, know how to give good gifts to…" spoke to me so deeply that it felt like if they were echoing in my mind. At that time I knew that God must have spoken directly to me. I might be an evil person, but I was not that bad that I would not give good things to those who needed it. And then it said, "how much more will your Father in heaven give the Holy Spirit to those who ask him!"

Still not understanding exactly what this was talking about, but still desperate for help and comfort, I said, "When you are speaking to me through these verses, please forgive me for the wrongs I have done and please send me the comforter, the Holy Spirit to help me through this storm."

KNOWN BEFORE BIRTH

After having done all this repenting and praying, I am not going to tell you that suddenly the waves stopped beating the ship, or that there was something else unusual going on in the cabin were I was staying. But something profound had happened in me. I felt a peace coming over me I had never experienced. My fear was gone, I was feeling that all things would become well. Promising God that the next harbor we would be in I would leave the ship to live for Him, I went to bed, and slept. It was kind of like in the story were Jesus was sleeping on the bottom of the boat, while the disciples were afraid that they might drown. (Mark 4:35-39). As the storm lasted for one more day I remember singing some of the Christian songs I had learned when I was a child, but when I came to points were I did not remember the words, other words; words that were kind of silly and without meaning to me at that time, started to come out of my mouth. And to my amazement, every time I did, these feelings of peace and joy followed motivating me to do it more and more. Of course, only when nobody was around.

Not until a couple of years later did I even learn the significance of this experience. I was while I was evangelizing in my home town one day when I met the guy who I was warned about because, they told me, he was an outspoken Pentecostal. Knowing this, I kept a wary eye on this individual, but he was friendly enough so we talked for awhile about our faith in Christ and the good things that God was doing for both of us. Then he asked me the question: was I baptized with the Holy Spirit when I accepted Jesus into my heart? Having been resolutely trained by the church of my youth that Pentecostals were demon-possessed, I could not help being on my guard. But, honestly I had never really looked into what this man was talking about, so I asked him to explain.

I listened with a swelling interest as he began to share some Bible verses with me, and to my surprise some of those verses he quoted were the same verses I had read on board of the ship. It was then, that I knew I was baptized with the Holy Spirit, and that when I sung silly songs, I was really singing in tongues. I had become a Pentecostal and I did not even know.

As we are talking about the Holy Spirit let me give you a Biblical introduction to better illustrate Him.

Beginning with the Trinity

There is one God manifested in three persons: the Father, the Son, and the Holy Spirit (I Timothy 3:16).

I think the term "trinity" more clearly indicates the "Three-in-One" aspect of the Godhead.

In Hebrew, the singular word for God is El, the dual tense is Elah, and to indicate three or more the word Elohim is used. Elohim is the word translated "God" in Genesis 1:1.

The Holy Spirit is a Person.

The Holy Spirit is thought by some to be an "essence" or "power" of God, rather than a separate person, because the Hebrew word for Spirit; Ruach, also means breath, and the Greek word for Spirit; Pneuma, also means wind or air.

We know He is a person.

The early Church scholar, Arias, caused division with his declaration that God the Father was the only true God. He maintained that Jesus was a created being, and the Holy Spirit was only an essence. This doctrine is known as the Arian heresy. Myriad scriptures show us the personhood of the Holy Spirit.

The Holy Spirit has the characteristics of a person

The Holy Spirit searches and has knowledge.–. I Corinthians 2:10-11
The Holy Spirit distributes gifts as He wills.–1 Corinthians 12:11
He has a mind.–Romans 8:27
He loves us.–Romans 15:30
He testifies of Jesus and exalts the Father and Son over Himself.–John 15:26, 16:13

Personal pronouns are used when referring to the Holy Spirit (John 1.4:16-17, John 16:7-15). "Comforter' in John 14:16 is "parakietos" which means "One who comes alongside of to help." The Holy Spirit is always with us ready to help when we ask Him to.

Personal acts are ascribed to the Holy Spirit.

The Holy Spirit speaks.–Acts 13:2
The Holy Spirit intercedes for us.–Romans 8:26
He teaches us.–1 John 2:20.27, John 14:26
The Holy Spirit guides Paul, sometimes forbidding things.–Acts 16:6.7
The Spirit strives with man.–. Genesis 6:3

The Holy Spirit can receive treatment as a person.

He can be grieved by us.–Ephesians 4:30
We can insult Him.–Hebrews 10:29
He can be lied to.–Acts 5:3
He can be blasphemed.–Matthew 12:31-32

The Holy Spirit is identified with the Father and the Son as a person.

He is named with the Father and Son in baptism.–Matthew 28:19
He is named with the Father and Son in benediction.–2 Corinthians 13:14
He is identified with the believers as a person.–Acts 15:28

The work of the Holy Spirit in the life of the Believer

The Holy Spirit is a helper who comes alongside us to guide us in our Christian walk (John 14:16).

The Holy Spirit is as important in a Christian's life as water for someone who is trying to shape a beautiful vase with his hands on a potters table. Without water to soften the clay, the material would be brittle, it would be impossible to give it the right shape no matter how much and how fast you would spin the table and the end product would be rough. Without the Holy Spirit in a Christian's life, we can come across to others as legalists, traditionalists and being religious. Without the Holy Spirit, we are not able to produce Godly fruit (John 15:4, 5), and we will lack God's anointing upon our ministries.

It is the Holy Spirit in ones live that makes it possible for a Christian to become the person God wants them to be.

The Holy Spirit is our Teacher (John 14.26, I John 2:27, I Corinthians 2: 13, 14).

When we are born again, we enter the dimension of the Spirit. In this dimension, we can be taught by Him to understand the things of God that are beyond the reach of our experience or intellect (2 Corinthians 4:18).

The Holy Spirit brings the Scriptures that we have read or heard to our remembrance (John 14:26). It is so good to have the right Scripture come to mind when we need it.

The Holy Spirit will guide us into all truth (John 16:12-13).

He will give us the discernment to judge between true and false teachings.
If we will open our hearts and read the Bible with the Spirit as our Guide, we will not stray from the truth and we will have all we need to live the Christian life (2 Peter 1:3).

The Holy Spirit will show us things to come (John 16:13).

The Spirit will help us to understand the prophecies in the books of Daniel and Revelation and Ezekiel. Since we are living in the last days, these prophecies are becoming more clear each day.

The Holy Spirit empowers the believer for service

"...All these are the work of one and the same Spirit, and he gives them to each one, just as he determines."–1 Corinthians 12:11

God also testified to it by signs, wonders and various miracles, and gifts of the Holy Spirit distributed according to his will.–Hebrews 2:4

Jesus said: *"I tell you the truth, anyone who has faith in me will do what*

I have been doing. He will do even greater things than these, because I am going to the Father."–John 14:12

The Promise of the Spirit

Acts 1:4-5 contains the promise by the Father to give the Holy Spirit to the believers.

In Joel 2:28, the Father said that in the last days He would pour out His Spirit upon all flesh.

The Power of the Spirit

In the book of Acts we learn that the Holy Spirit gives us the power to live the Christian life as a witness for God.

"... You will receive power when the Holy Spirit comes on you; and you will be my witnesses in Jerusalem, and in all Judea and Samaria, and to the ends of the earth."–Acts 1:8

It is impossible to live the Christian life without the power of the Spirit within us (Zechariah 4:6; John 15:4,5; Romans 7:15-25; Galatians 5:17-18; Matthew 26:41).

"Not by might nor by power, but by my Spirit," says the LORD Almighty.–Zechariah 4:6

To mention one of the great challenges I had to face as a Christian was my smoking habit. Truthfully, I LOVED smoking. I was the strangest paradigm you'd ever seen: the Marlboro-Man with a missionary badge, recognizable to friends by the cloud of smoke trailing behind and a passion for Jesus that made me smile as I preached. When I was not smoking regular cigarettes, I rolled my own. I smoked cigars, and pipes. I smoked them all to my hearts desire, and then I smoked some more. Sometimes I even emptied the ashtray of cigarette butts, filling my pipe just to keep the flavor in my mouth. Believe it or not, I thought it was so cool at the time, and deliriously I fooled myself into believing that it helped me think, or somehow made me more impervious to stress.

As a young Christian, just starting off in my walk of faith I was enveloped in a culture where many Christians smoked and none of them judged me or made a fuss about me smoking with them. But as I pursued people who were more sincere about their relationship with God and serious about growing spiritually I began to be attracted to a "Full Gospel" congregation and left behind the traditional church I had grown up in. Here my smoking started to raise some eyebrows. These people loved Jesus for sure. However, they weren't going to pull any punches for this issue in my life and were very apt to remind me that smoking was wrong. Not only this, but because my body was now the temple of God I was sinning. You can imagine how quickly I was to point out that since God created tobacco, there must be nothing wrong with it. For a while this argument made me confident, but soon the Holy Spirit started to deal with me. My response was, "Lord, I Love Smoking. I don't know if I can ever truthfully say that I don't like smoking. But when you want me to quit tobacco, you'd better change my desire for it." Several weeks after praying this, I finally gave it my first try to stop. Of course, I didn't do this without keeping some tobacco stashed away in my night stand, just in case I started to "need" some. But, God set me free and I haven't "needed" tobacco since. Now looking back, I hear stories from many other people who are trying hard to quit smoking. I am convinced that I could never have stopped smoking without the power of the Holy Spirit in my life.

The true witness lives his faith, believing that Jesus is with them.

Now faith is being sure of what we hope for and certain of what we do not see...And without faith it is impossible to please God, because anyone who comes to him must believe that he exists and that he rewards those who earnestly seek him.–Hebrews 11:1, 6;

Several years ago, my wife and I were invited by the A/G General Presbyter of a state called "Gujarath," to come to India. Though we were simply there for ministry, the trip was filled with adventures. We had just arrived, and were at the house of our host pastor that we met a friendly, nicely dressed Hindu man, who had found a book written by Dr. Robert Schuller of the Crystal Cathedral, located in California.

The theme of this book was becoming successful, and he wanted to know how it worked. The pastor, not knowing the book or the American writer, he asked me, just coming from America to spend some time with this Hindu visitor. Me, knowing about the writer but not knowing the book, I told him that the writer was a Christian, and he might have been writing about some Christian principles that would lead to successful living. I explained the scriptures, and then shared my personal testimony with him—accounting for how we were separated from God because of our sin, and how Jesus died on the cross, to take our sin away. Then I explained how Christ is constantly with believers, to help, comfort, and teach them by the power of the Holy Spirit. After I explained the part that Jesus was coming back again to take us home with Him to heaven. The man staring at the table was quiet for a while. I knew he was thinking about what had been said.

Finally looking at me and said, "This was great." He had never heard anyone explain it to him before. But then he asked this question, "Can you prove it?" To be honest with you, I was kind of taken by surprise to have him ask that question of me. Normally we just expect people to respond by accepting or rejecting the message. After thinking a brief second I answered him with "no, but I know somebody who can. May I pray for you?" After he responded by saying yes, I prayed, and asked none other than Jesus to introduce himself to this Hindu gentleman. And Jesus did. The next day, Sunday, he and his wife were in church, and both accepted Jesus in their heart, and together we had communion in remembrance of Jesus (1 Corinthians 11:17-34). It was a beautiful scene that could have never happened without the faith assurance that God would come through.

We need to believe that Jesus will be with us, and that He will confirm His Word with signs and wonders (Matthew 28:20b; Mark 16:20).

Before Peter received the power of the Holy Spirit, he was afraid to be identified with Jesus (Mark 14:53.72) even though he wanted to (Mark 14:27-31). After he received the power, he witnessed boldly to the same group of people who had tried Jesus (Acts 4:5.23), even telling them that there was no salvation apart from Christ. Then when Peter went back to the Christians, they prayed for greater boldness (v. 23—31).

Rather than trying to change the outside ourselves thinking that through that, we will change within. We must allow the Holy Spirit to change us within, (Romans 8). For a while, it may be possible for a person to change the behavioral output of his life on his own, and still have the same unrighteous attitudes and desires inside. But, living for Christ is not merely a behavioral issue. It is deeper even to the very heart of mankind. True transformation can never occur by man's own strength. As we yield each area of our lives to the Spirit, He conforms us into the image of Christ.

In all my prayers for all of you, I always pray with joy because of your partnership in the gospel from the first day until now, being confident of this, that he who began a good work in you will carry it on to completion until the day of Christ Jesus.–Philippians 1:4-6

While the gifts of the Spirit are valuable and necessary, Paul recommends the fruit of the Spirit as "a more excellent way" in I Corinthians 12:31, following this encouragement with a whole chapter about the most important fruit. It is the love chapter–1 Corinthians 13.

The Gifts of the Holy Spirit

Because of an over-generalized use of the word "gift," much confusion has arisen in the area of spiritual gifts. The following is set forth to clarify and simplify some of the confusion and to aid in determining individual spiritual gifts. It is not intended to be an exhaustive study, but merely to be a guide to the subject.

Classification of "gifts"

Before there can be any discussion as to what the spiritual gifts are; we must review how they have been viewed in scripture.

In 1 Corinthians 12:1-7, the Apostle Paul discusses spiritual matters (the word "gifts" in verse 1 is a supplied word). Verse 4 speaks of "diversities of gifts," verse 5 speaks of differences of administrations, and verse 6 refers to "diversities of operations."

The Berkeley version of the Bible translates the Greek here as distinctive gifts of grace, "distinctive ministries" and "varieties of things accomplished," respectively.

From this, 3 basic classifications have been derived:
(1) Motivational gifts: **(2)** Ministries: and **(3)** Manifestations.

Each Christian is given one gift of grace also known as a motivational gift, which is his viewpoint on life. Christians may have many ministries in varying degrees. Manifestations of the Spirit are determined solely by God the Holy Spirit and are a result rather than a gift.

This study will concentrate on the motivational gifts which are listed in Romans l2:5-8 and their brief descriptions are listed respectively in verses 9 through 15 of the same chapter.

Spiritual gifts

If each Christian properly understood his spiritual gift, it would not only motivate him to greater commitment and service, but would also bring a whole new excitement to the Body of Christ.

Every Spirit filled Christian has a spiritual gift

When we were born physically we possessed certain natural abilities. When we were born again spiritually, we received certain spiritual abilities as a member of the Body of Christ. "So we being many are one body in Christ and everyone members one of another Having then gifts differing according to the grace that was given us…Romans 12:5,6

Joy comes in exercising our gift

The root word for gift is "Charisma." This comes from the word CHAR which means joy. "Charis" is the word for grace which involves God giving us the desire and power to accomplish God's will. (Phil. 2:13).

Finding personal fulfillment is only possible by developing our spiritual gift

Each of us has a desire for meaningful achievement. The ultimate of this is having a significant part in a divine program. This divine program is being carried through the Body of Christ by the proper functioning of each man's gift.

Each gift is designed to perfect the body of Christ

Just as there are varying functions in the members of our body, so each Christian has a particular and necessary function in the Body of Christ. Failure to exercise our gift weakens the ministry of the Body of Christ.

God wants each of us to understand our gift

If we are to concentrate on our gift as instructed in Romans 12, we must first understand what that gift is. Also, if we are to have harmony with others within the Body of Christ, we must understand what their particular functions are.

There are seven basic motivations

1. Declaring truth. **2.** Serving. **3.** Teaching. **4.** Exhorting
5. Giving. **6.** Ruling (Administration). **7.** Empathizing (Mercy)

The following scripture indicates that we have only one basic motivational gift

"...As every man hath received the gift, even so minister the same to one another."

The noun for gift in I Peter 4:10 is singular in number.

Gifts are compared to members of a body. "For we have many members in one body and all members have not the same office, so we being many are one body in Christ." Rom.12:4

Each man is to concentrate fully on the gift God has given him. This would not be possible if he had more than one motivational gift. *(See Romans 12:3-8)*

Knowing each other's motivation coordinates and unifies Christians within the body of Christ

If a chairman of a church board has the motivation of serving, he will emphasize practical needs. If a pastor has the gift of mercy he will emphasize the feelings of people through his messages and prayers. If a pastor has the motivation of administration, he will emphasize getting projects completed and proper procedure to accomplish the projects.

Purpose of our gift:

Discovering blind spots
When another Christian sees us, he will tend to evaluate us on the basis of his strong points. (He will judge us on the basis of his weak points. Romans 2:1-3) With his evaluation there will be a strong desire to help us achieve in the areas he has already learned. In order not to think of ourselves more highly than we ought to think *(Romans 12:3)* we must go to the following for counsel regarding our blind spots:

Prophesy: To reveal motives and actions which are ungodly.
Service: To see areas of service which you overlooked and attitudes of ungratefulness.
Teaching: To explain inaccuracies of statements or conclusions which you have made.
Exhortation: To pinpoint causes of problems and steps of solution.
Giving: To reveal unwise use of assets.
Administration: To point out mismanagement of time or procedure in accomplishing goals.
Mercy: To share areas of insensitivity.

Fulfilling responsibilities

We are to put our whole heart and soul into whatever we do. (Colossians 3:22) In order to do this, we should visualize how this activity can be an expression of our motivational gift.

If we have the gift of mercy, but a responsibility to be a teacher, we must view the teaching job as a means of promoting harmony and understanding.

Determining priorities

It may be that we have assumed responsibilities which God did not intend us to have or activities which detract from our ability to concentrate on our gift. We are instructed in Romans 12 to concentrate on whatever our gift is. This concentration is required so that we will be able to make a significant contribution to the cause of Christ through the motivation that God has given to us.

Delegating responsibilities

By knowing what our gift is, we should have a new freedom and ability to delegate responsibilities to others whose spiritual motivation would better equip them for achievement.

Anticipating responses

By knowing what the motivations of others are and learning to see situations from

their point of view, we will be able to anticipate and understand their responses. (Philippians 2:4) We will further be able to harmonize their responses and gain the value of the emphasis which God is seeking to make through them.

Edifying the body of Christ

We have a strong desire to see every other Christian learn the skills which we emphasize through our gift. As we learn how to share with them our motivation, we are not only developing a life message, but we are expressing the love of Christ and perfecting His body. (1 Peter. 4:10)

If we fail to exercise our gift in this way, there will be weakness and imbalance in the church.

All of us might have different gifts; however each of us is commanded to perform all seven activities

Declaring truth: "Make love your aim and earnestly desire spiritual gifts especially that you may prophesy (proclaim truth)." I Corinthians 14:1

Serving: "Through love serve one another." Galatians 5:13. "Whatever you do, do your work heartily, as for the Lord…It is the Lord Christ whom ye serve." Colossians 3:23-24

Teaching: "Teach and help one another along the right road with your psalms and hymns and spiritual songs…" Colossians 3:16. "…Teach them to observe all things that I have commanded you." Matthew 28:20

Exhorting: "Exhort one another daily, while it is called today." Hebrews 3:13.
"…Exhorting one another: and so much the more, as ye see the day approaching. Heb. 10:25

Giving: "Freely ye have received, freely give." Matt. 10:3 "Give and it shall be given unto you…" Luke 6:38. "Distribute to the necessity of the saints." Rom 12:13.

Ruling: "A father must manage his own household well." I Tim. 3:4. "A wise servant shall have rule over a son that causes shame, and shall have part of the inheritance among the brethren." Proverbs 17:2. "…He that rules his spirit is mightier than he that takes a city." Proverbs 16:32.

Mercy: After illustrating mercy in the account of the good Samaritan, Jesus said, "Go and do likewise."–Luke 10:37. "Bear ye one another's burdens and so fulfill the law of Christ."–2 Cor. 13:8. "…put on a heart of compassion,"–Col. 3:12

The fruit of the Holy Spirit

But the fruit of the Spirit is love, joy, peace, patience, kindness, goodness, faithfulness, gentleness and self-control.–Galatians 5:22, 23

The visible life of a disciple must show clearly that he is a follower of Jesus Christ. Others should be able to see in his life the fruit of the Holy Spirit of God. In practice a disciple must live out the reality of what Paul talks about. Personally, I believe that we can say we are filled with the Holy Spirit, we can assume the office assigned to us by the Holy Spirit, we can fan into flame the gifts of the Holy Spirit, and see manifestations following, but when the fruit of the Holy Spirit is not present (which Paul describes as the "most excellent way), we need to ask ourselves what spirit is truly in control at the moment. For example: As we consider what it means to be filled with the Holy Spirit, we can think about a sponge which soaks up whatever liquid it is placed in. Now imagine for a moment that a sponge is dunked into a bucket of red dyed water. Within seconds that sponge is saturated and filled. When someone would take the sponge out of the bucket, and squeeze it, hit it with a baseball bat or throw it against a white painted wall, you will find out that red dye will come out of that sponge and leave it's mark. There will be no lime green or baby blue; only red, which is the evidence that it has been in the bucket to begin with. I believe the same thing will happen with the Christian who is filled with the living water from God. When the world applies pressure to us or persecutes us nothing should come out but the fruit of the Holy Spirit if we are truly residing in Christ. His presence in us will show, and will be felt by those around us.

The spiritual process of a seed being planted, growing, being pruned, and reaching maturity is all to the ends of producing fruit. Jesus said, "Thus, by their fruit you will recognize them" (Matthew 7:20). The evidence that we belong to Jesus is in what we are producing and others see, not the manifestations of miracles or leadership ability. I believe that it is the fruit of the Holy Spirit in one's live that validates the fact that the Holy Spirit is in control.

"But the fruit of the Spirit is love *(agape)*" (Galatians *5:22).* The fruit of the Spirit defines the supernatural love and Character of God.

Joy is love's consciousness. When we love, we are so filled with joy that even normally miserable tasks are pleasurable.

Peace is more than the cessation of hostilities. Love that wishes no ill is the basis for true peace.

Longsuffering is the characteristic of love that makes us kind after being continually mistreated, without keeping track of the offenses.

Love is gentle, not harsh or abrasive.

Love is the only positive motive for goodness. Some people are "good" because they fear the consequences of doing something wrong, but that is not true goodness.

The faith mentioned in this verse is not the gift of the Spirit listed in I Corinthians 12:9, but is a loving trust in people

Meekness does not vaunt itself and does not seek praise and honor.

Temperance is moderation.

These characteristics of agape love are the result of the Holy Spirit's work in our lives

To have others taste the fruit of the Holy Spirit, will cause them to want to belong to Him.

We can see this happen in the Holy Spirit filled early church;

They lived a holy and righteous lifestyle. (Acts 19:18, 19)
"And they ceased not to teach and preach Jesus Christ."–Acts 5:41-42
"God added to the church daily"–Acts 2:47

They were encouraged to *"Fan into flame the gifts of God"*–2 Tim. 2:6
And God worked with them *confirming His word* with signs and wonders....

* I believe, reading the scriptures, that, Pentecost is for all who wish to have it.
* We will never reach our generation with the Gospel message until we have experienced a personal Pentecost—Just as those in the book of Acts.

The reason for not having the fruit of the Spirit:

"Do not grieve the Holy Spirit of God, with whom you were sealed for the day of redemption"–Ephesians 4:30

Not bearing fruit results when a relationship with Jesus Christ and the Holy Spirit is not as it should be. A Christian may trust Jesus Christ for his salvation, but when he is living in sin, he is therefore not under the control of the Holy Spirit. The presence of sin in a life takes away the evidence that the Holy Spirit is there.

James warned that it is impossible for the person who claims to be a Christian, but lives in sin to manifest the fruit of the Holy Spirit of God. He was speaking about the use of their tongues, but the same truth applies to every aspect of a Christian's life.

"With the tongue we praise our Lord and Father, and with it we curse men, who have been made in God's likeness. Out of the same mouth come praise and cursing. My brothers, this should not be. Can both fresh water and salt water flow from the same spring? My brothers, can a fig tree bear olives, or a grapevine bear figs? Neither can a salt spring produce fresh water."–James 3:9-12

God will not manifest fruit through the Holy Spirit in the life of a person who is rebellious against his authority and still has self on the throne of his life. God simply won't show his presence in a person who wants to go his own way. *"For rebellion is like the sin of divination, and arrogance like the evil of idolatry"–1 Samuel 15:23*.

The key issue is lordship; the Christian is not allowing Jesus Christ to be

Lord of his life. Christians, who have not submitted to the lordship of Jesus, are really not his disciples. They may have received him as Savior, but not as Lord. A disciple has a dynamic relationship with God, demonstrating attractively the fruit of the Spirit.

In general people want to copy the images and lifestyles of others that seem attractive to them. Just look at the fashion world, and think about how we feel drawn to get certain clothes to wear.

As a Christian, all we have to do is look around in our church, in Christian organizations, in our job, and in society to find men and women who are living attractive Christian lives. We can't help but be challenged by them. We want to be like them. But we should follow them only as they are following Jesus Christ.

The Apostle Paul wrote to a church which was having some difficulties in this area: *"Follow my example, as I follow the example of Christ"–1 Corinthians 11:1*. Paul followed the example of the most attractive life the world has seen.

In another letter Paul wrote, *"Whatever you have learned or received or heard from me, or seen in me, put it into practice" Philippians 4:9*. Paul had an attractive relationship with Jesus Christ which was visible, as evidenced by the crowds that followed him. The Apostle Peter tells us to *"grow in the grace and knowledge of our Lord and Savior Jesus Christ"–2 Peter 3:18*.

In his earlier letter he was asked: But how is it to your credit if you receive a beating for doing wrong and endure it? But if you suffer for doing good and you endure it, this is commendable before God. To this you were called, because Christ suffered for you, leaving you an example, that you should follow in his steps (1 Peter 2:20-21).

The Apostle Paul challenged our thinking when he pointed out that *"those God foreknew he also predestined to be conformed to the likeness of his Son"–Romans 8:29*.

Our destiny is that we be conformed to the likeness of Jesus Christ. Because of that mature believers will have a tremendous appeal to all. In contrast to those who live in sin, Paul tells us to *"clothe yourselves with the*

Lord Jesus Christ, and do not think about how to gratify the desires of the sinful nature"–Romans 13:14.

No matter how reluctant they are to admit it, unbelievers are attracted to Christians who follow Jesus. This was the case when the apostles Peter and John were brought before the Sanhedrin, the ruling body of the Jews. Even the unsaved members of this ecclesiastical body recognized unusual courage and knew that these men had been with Jesus. Peter and John were bearing fruit to that fact, and that was attractive even to the Sanhedrin.

We cannot develop the fruit of the Spirit in our own strength.

It comes only through the relationship with the indwelling Holy Spirit. If we give ourselves to walking in the power of the Holy Spirit, He will produce the needed fruit in us. We must give complete control of our body, mind, and soul to Christ, and let him demonstrate his power in and through us.

Christians who are developing the fruit of the Holy Spirit live in diligence.

The Apostle Peter had this to say about our responsibility:

"For this very reason, make every effort to add to your faith goodness; and to goodness, knowledge; and to knowledge, self-control; and to self-control, perseverance; and to perseverance, godliness; and to godliness, brotherly kindness; and to brotherly kindness, love. For if you possess these qualities in increasing measure, they will keep you from being ineffective and unproductive in your knowledge of our Lord Jesus Christ."–2 Peter 1:5-8

We are to "make every effort!" If we have problems with self-control, for example, then it is our responsibility to learn how we might best govern our actions. The Holy Spirit will provide the strength we lack. The same is true with the other qualities.

How to receive the Baptism of the Holy

While Apollos was at Corinth, Paul took the road through the interior and arrived at Ephesus. There he found some disciples and asked them, "Did you receive the Holy Spirit when you believed?" They answered, "No, we have not even heard that there is a Holy Spirit." So Paul asked, "Then what baptism did you receive?" "John's baptism," they replied. Paul said, "John's baptism was a baptism of repentance. He told the people to believe in the one coming after him, that is, in Jesus." On hearing this, they were baptized into the name of the Lord Jesus. When Paul placed his hands on them, the Holy Spirit came on them, and they spoke in tongues and prophesied.–Acts 19:1-6

To receive the Holy Spirit, we need to welcome Him. This means that we need to:

Believe in Jesus Christ.–John 3:14-16
Just as Moses lifted up the snake in the desert, so the Son of Man must be lifted up, that everyone who believes in him may have eternal life. For God so loved the world that he gave his one and only Son, that whoever believes in him shall not perish but have eternal life.

Repent from your worldly lifestyle.–Acts 2:38-39
Peter replied, "Repent and be baptized, every one of you, in the name of Jesus Christ for the forgiveness of your sins. And you will receive the gift of the Holy Spirit. . The promise is for you and your children and for all who are far off—for all whom the Lord our God will call."

Be born again–belong to Jesus–Romans 8:9;
You, however, are controlled not by the sinful nature but by the Spirit, if the Spirit of God lives in you. And if anyone does not have the Spirit of Christ, he does not belong to Christ.

Earnestly long to be filled–Matthew 6:33
But seek first his kingdom and his righteousness, and all these things will be given to you as well.

Desire to be filled for God's glory and not our own
Example of Jesus: Luke 22:42
"Father, if you are willing, take this cup from me; yet not my will, but yours be done."

Just Ask–Luke 11:11
"Which of you fathers, if your son asks for a fish, will give him a snake instead? Or if he asks for an egg, will give him a scorpion? If you then, though you are evil, know how to give good gifts to your children, how much more will your Father in heaven give the Holy Spirit to those who ask him!"

You need to believe in the promise–Galatians 3:2; James 1:6-8
"But when he asks, he must believe and not doubt, because he who doubts is like a wave of the sea, blown and tossed by the wind. That man should not think he will receive anything from the Lord; he is a double-minded man, unstable in all he does."

Surrender–Present your bodies as a living sacrifice–Romans 12:1,2
"Therefore, I urge you, brothers, in view of God's mercy, to offer your bodies as living sacrifices, holy and pleasing to God—this is your spiritual act of worship. Do not conform any longer to the pattern of this world, but be transformed by the renewing of your mind. Then you will be able to test and approve what God's will is—his good, pleasing and perfect will."

Be willing to be emptied out of everything else.–James 4:3
"When you ask, you do not receive, because you ask with wrong motives, that you may spend what you get on your pleasures."

Be willing to obey–Acts 5:32
"We are witnesses of these things, and so is the Holy Spirit, whom God has given to those who obey him."

Yield wholly to God and His will.–1 Peter 4:1-2

"Therefore, since Christ suffered in his body, arm yourselves also with the same attitude, because he who has suffered in his body is done with sin. As a result, he does not live the rest of his earthly life for evil human desires, but rather for the will of God."

Exercise your gifts. 1 Peter 4:10

"Each one should use whatever gift he has received to serve others, faithfully administering God's grace in its various forms."

5. Sharing Your Faith

But you will receive power when the Holy Spirit comes on you; and you will be my witnesses in Jerusalem, and in all Judea and Samaria, and to the ends of the earth."–Jesus (Acts 1:8)

As I shared in my testimony in this book's introduction, I had my first real known encounter with Jesus while I was desperate for His help. That moment fearing death, what it would be like to drown and then go to hell afterwards caused me to cry out to God, hoping for a miracle. Well, I now praise God everyday, because I received my miracle! Jesus spoke to me through His word. He affirmed me with His love for me. He saved me, forgave me, and filled me with the Holy Spirit, and I learned for the first time in my life what it was to have genuine peace. The first harbor town we entered I told the captain I was leaving the ship, and then took a twelve hour train ride back from Kiel, Germany to my home town, which was located a little north of Amsterdam in the Netherlands.

I knew that that was the thing for me to do, even though for me it was a step into the unknown. Something had happened to me. It was perhaps kind of strange for me, but somehow while on the train, I felt the strong need to tell my experience to some one. I found my self praying, "Lord put someone on that seat in front of me, so I can tell them what happened to me." And God did. The next twelve hours I had the chance to tell my story to all who chose to sit in the seat at that one bench facing me. In spite of the fact that I had no experience in doing what I was doing, people listened, and people responded prayerfully to the Gospel message. Of course coming back into my home town, they thought it strange that I had left the ship, and that I had become a radical Christian. The fact that I had an encounter with Jesus was hard to swallow, especially among those who were still going to the same church were I had left to be a sailor. They did not understand that someone could have an experience that made you so excited about God that you had to tell everybody about it. My adventure with Jesus had begun. And before long I was involved in street evangelism, using what ever tools I had available to me and people got saved on a daily basis.

But in your hearts set apart Christ as Lord. Always be prepared to give an answer to everyone who asks you to give the reason for the hope that you have. But do this with gentleness and respect, keeping a clear conscience, so that those who speak maliciously against your good behavior in Christ may be ashamed of their slander.–1 Peter 3:15,16

Being zealous for God

"...Jesus Christ; who gave himself for us, that he might redeem us from all iniquity, and purify unto himself a people for his own possession, zealous of good works."–Titus 2:14

Since I read it the first time, I have always been fascinated with the story found in Luke 24, where after the death and burial of Jesus, the disciples were talking about the things that had happened, "with their faces downcast" (vs.17). How they did not recognize Jesus as he walked and talked among them. But then, see their response when they did recognize Him. They were so excited about their encounter that they asked each other, *"Were not our hearts burning within us while he talked with us on the road and opened the Scriptures to us?"* They got up and returned at once to Jerusalem.– Luke 24:32,33.

It seems that suddenly they forgot how hungry and tired they were. They forgot that it was getting dark and dangerous on the road. They had only one thought, "Let's go, and tell the others." I personally believe that this happens with us too, when we have an encounter with Jesus. We too want to go and tell others of his plan for us full of love, mercy, grace. I believe that a spirit-filled, born again believer ought to be ready at all times to communicate the gospel.

Evangelism is the key to disciple making and must be the cutting edge of any lasting ministry.

In every form of ministry with which my wife and I have been involved, we always kept evangelism in the forefront, while continually striving to combine it with good mentoring and discipleship. Looking at the life of the Apostle Paul, he always followed up and discipled the men he had won to Christ, but he never forsook evangelizing. And so must we. Evangelism and Discipleship belongs to go hand in hand with each other, knowing that at the same time they will bring new life into a ministry.

And the Lord added to their number daily those who were being saved.–Acts 2:42-47

The reason for this growth?

In Acts we read that people were constantly being reached with the gospel. What was their reason for this? Those who began that ministry in the first church never lost their vision for evangelism. Evangelism must not just be an exercise, but must be the lifestyle of the disciple. To help you get started in this adventure, let me give you some basic ideas and strategies that could help get you going.

The evangelism of Christian men and women in the early Church was characterized by at least three things For example read Acts 19:1-20

The name of the Lord was magnified.

(Vs. 17) The name of the Lord Jesus was held in high honor. They respected God, and the things they knew were important to God, and lived accordingly. (Read: Acts 2:41-47)

There was a genuine act of repentance among them.

(Vs. 18) Many of those who believed now came and openly confessed their evil deeds. They publicly testified and the burning of superstitious books / charms took place.

Acts 5:42; They openly identified with Jesus Christ. Everywhere they went and in anything they did, they were not ashamed to be identified with the Savior.

"Day after day, in the temple courts and from house to house, they never stopped teaching and proclaiming the good news that Jesus is the Christ"

The word of the Lord spread widely and grew in power. (Vs.20)

They demonstrated the presence, and the fruit of the Spirit, while pursuing Holiness and righteousness. There was something in their lives that drew other people to them. Others, including their enemies, knew that they had been with Jesus. *"When they saw the courage of Peter and John and realized that they were unschooled, ordinary men, they were astonished and they took note that these men had been with Jesus"–Acts 4:13.*

They were actively seeking to influence other people toward Jesus Christ. We read that right after the persecution the church scattered to other areas of the Near East. Luke tells us, *"Now those who had been scattered by the persecution in connection with Stephen traveled as far as Phoenicia, Cyprus and Antioch, telling the message only to Jews"–Acts 11:19.* Then men from Cyprus and Cyrene began sharing the gospel with non-Jews, *"and a great number of people believed and turned to the Lord"–Acts 11:21.* And God worked with them confirming His Word with signs and wonders.

Let's remember the Words of Jesus: *"He who is not with me is against me, and he who does not gather with me scatters.–Matthew 12:30.*

The importance of knowing your testimony

Successful evangelism generally begins with a well prepared testimony, in which a person shares what Jesus Christ has done in his own personal life, not only what he has heard about God doing in someone else's life.

Ministering in the western world, I've found that many people, particularly those raised in Christian homes and Bible-believing churches, feel they have no testimony to share. But the truth of the matter is that all of us have a testimony. Not everyone may have a dramatic "life or death" story to tell, but there is change in every one of us nevertheless. Giving God the glory for this change is definitely powerful!

Any time the grace of God touches a life there is a story to tell.

As a core of our evangelism training, we require that every person write out his or her testimony, and find someone to share it with. The testimony has four basic points:

What that person's life was like before he met the Savior?
How that person came to know that he had eternal life;
How God has answered your prayers
Write about the benefits of knowing Jesus Christ since conversion.

Every born-again, Spirit-filled Christian should be able to write out a testimony. No matter where you are, you should be able to communicate the gospel of Jesus Christ through your testimony. A commitment to the primacy of evangelism is a must for the growing Christian disciple.

Testimony examples found in the Bible

The Bible gives us some clear testimonies. Two of Paul's sermons were nothing more than a retelling of how he met Jesus Christ. The first testimony was given to the mob of Jews that had just tried to lynch him. Paul began with what his life was like before he met the Lord in a moving and powerful way drawing a sharp contrast to his new life:

"The Jews all know the way I have lived ever since I was a child, from the beginning of my life in my own country, and also in Jerusalem. They have known me for a long time and can testify, if they are willing, that according to the strictest sect of our religion, I lived as a Pharisee..." "I too was convinced that I ought to do all that was possible to oppose the name of Jesus of Nazareth. And that is just what I did in Jerusalem. On the authority of the chief priests I put many of the saints in prison, and when they were put to death, I cast my vote against them. Many a time I went from one synagogue to another to have them punished, and I tried to force them to blaspheme. In my obsession against them, I even went to foreign cities to persecute them"–Acts 26:4-5, 9-11.

Then Paul shared how he actually came to know the Savior:

"On one of these journeys I was going to Damascus with the authority and commission of the chief priests. About noon, O king, as I was on the road, I saw a light from heaven, brighter than the sun, blazing around me and my companions. We all fell to the ground, and I heard a voice saying to me in Aramaic, 'Saul, Saul, why do you persecute me? It is hard for you to kick against the goads.' Then I asked, 'Who are you, Lord?' 'I am Jesus, whom you are persecuting,' the Lord replied. 'Now get up and stand on your feet. I have appeared to you to appoint you as a servant and as a witness of what you have seen of me and what I will show you. I will rescue you from your own people and from the Gentiles. I am sending you to open their eyes and turn them from darkness to light, and from the power of Satan to God, so that they may receive forgiveness of sins and a place among those who are sanctified by faith in me.'"–Acts 26:12-18

Finally, Paul told his audience what the Lord meant to him in his present life:

"So then, King Agrippa, I was not disobedient to the vision from heaven. First to those in Damascus, then to those in Jerusalem and in all Judea, and to the Gentiles also, I preached that they should repent and turn to God and prove their repentance by their deeds. That is why the Jews seized me in the temple courts and tried to kill me. But I have had God's help to this very day, and so I stand here and testify to small and great alike. I am saying nothing beyond what the prophets and Moses said would happen—that the Christ would suffer and, as the first to rise from the dead, would proclaim light to his own people and to the Gentiles."–Acts 26:19-23

Your testimony is your authority to speak about Christ and His message

We find another excellent example of a testimony in the early Church as described in Acts 4. Peter and John had come to the temple in Jerusalem to pray. On the way in, they had healed a man who had been born lame. After they had preached to the crowd that gathered, they were arrested and taken before the Sanhedrin, the ruling religious body of the Jews (see Acts 4:13-14).

Two things stand out here. The men in the Sanhedrin recognized that Peter and John had been with the Lord. They also saw the testimony of the former lame man, and had nothing to say. He had been lame and God had healed him through Peter and John. The testimony of two courageous lives and the testimony of a changed life were indeed powerful. After the Sanhedrin threatened the two men they were released, but immediately Peter and John went back to prayer. Note what they asked for:

"Now, Lord, consider their threats and enable your servants to speak your word with great boldness."–Acts 4:29

Boldness in Christ makes us forget about our worldly pride so we are unashamed to talk about Jesus Christ, and makes unembarrassed freedom of speech possible. Here in this scripture, Peter and John were praying for freedom to proclaim the Gospel of Jesus Christ.

God answered the prayer of Peter and John instantly.

"After they prayed, the place where they were meeting was shaken. And they were all filled with the Holy Spirit and spoke the word of God boldly."–Acts 4:31

They went out and did what they were supposed to do in the power of the Holy Spirit, who enables us to witness and give our testimony effectively.

A well told testimony can make a great impact on people.

When the person with whom you have shared your testimony continues to be interested, you must now present the simple gospel story from the Scriptures so that he can come to a saving knowledge of Jesus Christ. For this you need a plan for a clear gospel presentation.

Some of the Advantages of a Plan

It enables you to be prepared at all times to witness. You are able to answer anyone who wants to know how to come to Jesus Christ.

It enables you to go through a biblical presentation point by point without leaving anything out. You will have covered everything vital to that person's coming to Jesus Christ.

It serves as a set of tracks that provide direction. If the person with whom you are sharing the Lord takes off on a tangent, having a plan enables you to come back to where you ought to be after you have taken care of the diversion.

It is a transferable tool by which you can teach others to share Christ as well.

Sharing important Gospel truths.

The following words found in scripture are to give new meaning to life:.

Sin. We begin with the fact that all of us are infected with sin, and separated from God. "All have sinned and fall short of the glory of God..." (Romans 3:10-18; 23.)

Death. Sin leads to death, which is the penalty of sin. (Romans 5:12; 6:23).

Ransom. Because God is righteous and holy, he cannot overlook our sins. Someone has to pay for them. (Hebrews 9:27; Exodus 34:6-7). Someone else has paid for our sin and is our deliverer from sins and their penalty. The penalty has already been paid by Jesus Christ on the cross of Calvary. (Romans 5:8; Isaiah 53:6; 1 Peter 2:24).

Grace. The Bible declares that this salvation cannot be earned, for it is a free gift from God to those who accept it by faith. Redemption is all of grace, absolutely free. (Ephesians 2:8-9; Titus 3:5; Romans 3:24).

Repentance. We need to acknowledge truth; Believe in God's Word; and confess our sin. "He who covers up his sins does not prosper, but whoever confesses and renounces them finds mercy." (Proverbs 28:13; 1 John 1:9)

Deliverance. Our deliverance comes when we receive Jesus Christ into our life by a prayer of commitment to him. (Revelation 3:20; John 1:12; Romans 10:9-10).

When a person understands what the Bible teaches and has received the Savior by faith, he needs to be assured that God indeed has saved him. So we need to conclude a successful gospel presentation by sharing with the convert some assurance verses. Some of the Scriptures that give this assurance are John 5:24, 1 John 5:11-13, John 10:28, Hebrews 7:25, and 1 Timothy 1:12.

The Holy Spirit. In order to grow spiritually we need to Holy Spirit in or lives, for without Him we can't do anything. (Zechariah 4:6; John 15:4, 5)

Some Practical Evangelism Strategies to Consider:

Community evangelism

When Jesus sent out His disciples (Read: Luke 10:1-16), he gave them several instructions which can be very useful for us as well. They can give us confidence and direction, in our mission of reaching the world for Christ.

Each disciple was told by Jesus to do the following things:

Jesus sent them out in pairs of two. (vs. 2)
This concept builds power of unity, accountability, and protection, but each one can also be an encouragement to the other. Being sent out in pairs also agrees with what Jesus said in Matthew:

"I tell you the truth, whatever you bind on earth will be bound in Heaven, and whatever you loose on earth will be loosed in Heaven. Again, I tell you that if two of you on earth agree about anything you ask for, it will be done for you by My Father in Heaven. For where two or three come together in my name, there am I with them."–Matt. 18:18-20

He told His disciples to pray for more workers. (vs. 2)
"The harvest is plentiful, but the workers are few"...Keep in mind, harvest time is just a short season, and the job to be done is bigger than just a few people can handle. Like the summer harvest season, life is fleeting, and without people busy showing the love of Christ to all the world many opportunities to reap souls out of death will be lost. Until the Lord's return, every generation has a harvest season.

Jesus warned His disciples to be wise, tactful, and cautious and to use discernment. (vs. 3)
"Go, I am sending you out like lambs among wolves. In Matt. 10:16, Jesus said, "Be as shrewd as snakes and as innocent as doves."

Jesus wanted the disciples to concentrate on their task, and to trust in Him who sent them. (vs. 4) Do not let yourself be sidetracked by your needs, but utilize each moment to its fullest potential. There is only limited time.

Jesus said "stay put" (vs. 7)
"Do not move around from house to house." Jesus wanted them to minister stability, and consistency demonstrating that they were available to disciple those who responded to the Gospel message. This principle promotes the ministry of church planting, or home/cell groups.

Jesus told them to bring peace and minister healing. (vs. 5, 9)
He said, "Say peace to this house and heal the sick." Jesus wants His disciples to minister wholeness, restoration and reconciliation to humanity, seeing to it that healing is supernaturally brought to physical, spiritual and emotional needs.

Jesus told His disciples to be straight in their message. (vs. 10-11)
Do not compromise, be strong, tell the message as it is, and let people decide for themselves how they want to respond. When there is a negative response, move on, do not argue!

Believe in your message–personal testimony. (vs. 11)
"Yet be sure of this, the Kingdom is near."–Speak out of conviction–Do not be discouraged when some people don't respond. Do not stop!!! Gal. 6:9 reads, "Do not grow weary in doing good, for at the proper time, we will reap a harvest if we do not give up" (Read also I Corinthians. 15:58)

Remember to remind others of the results of unbelief (vs. 12-15)
Romans 6:23 reads; "For the wages of sin is death…, But the free gift of God is eternal life in Christ, Jesus our Lord."

Do not forget, it's about accepting or rejecting Jesus Christ (vs. 16)
When people respond negatively…do not take it personally! Pray for them. We can do this without their permission and cooperation! Let us reach out for Jesus.

Practical Friendship Evangelism

According to statistics, at least 80% of those who accept Jesus Christ as their personal Savior, do so because a friend either invited them to an evangelistic event, or because a friend gave them a personal witness or testimony. Therefore it is very important for each of us to develop a personal plan for evangelism that will call us to action.

Here are six easy steps to follow which will challenge you to bear fruit as God enables:

Prayerfully select one to three friends, colleagues or neighbors who are not Christians. Make it a mandate to pray for them on a regular daily basis, and ask God how you can be a witness to them. Write their names somewhere you will see them everyday.

Identify three ways to build a "bridge" with each individual, which shows them that you care and that they know you are interested in them and in their lives. Be aware, "People don't care how much you know, until they know how much you care."

The Apostle Paul wrote in I Corinthians 9:19-22; *"for though I am free from all men. I have made myself a slave to all, that I might win the more"... "To the weak, I became weak, that I might win the weak; I have become all things to all men, that I may by all means save some."*

Choose three "events" for each individual named that will build on step #2 and give you quality time with your friends. A variety of different events can be very helpful, however, make sure that your friend will be exposed to the Gospel of Christ in an appropriate way in at least one of the events.

Plan for three different times where you will have an opportunity to share a "personal testimony" with them. These testimonies may be different from one another depending on the person, the need and the situation he/she might find him/herself in. These testimonies need prayerful thought and preparation. (Watch out...don't preach, or use Christian "lingo"!)

"Counting the cost"-Think about having a personal mission's budget. Think about a creative way to save money for your evangelism outreach. An example could be that at the end of every day you put all your change in a cookie jar, so that when the time is right you have the money needed to cover any expenses involved with your personal mission's project.

A prayer support team is very important. Try to find people within your church who would like to be prayer partners with you. These individuals need to be the kind who will encourage you and hold you accountable to your plan for evangelism. The best prospects would be those who share common goals and have developed their own personal plan for evangelism.

Please be encouraged to involve one of the pastoral staff members from your church. A regular (once a month) time to pray together will also prove beneficial. Remember: only the Holy Spirit can and will open hardened hearts. You are only asked to be obedient and witness. The results are up to Him.

Ministering to our Muslim Neighbor

Many people from the Muslim culture are looking for answers, just like we are. And out of experience we have learned that they are very open to the things of God. We need to understand that even though many Muslims are born into a Muslim nation, or family, that does not necessarily make them a Muslim believer. It is the same with us. Being born in a Christian home does not make us automatically a Christian

The following are some practical suggestions how to witness to our Muslim neighbor.

Pray the fullest blessing of Christ on them whether they love you or not.

Bless those who curse you, pray for those who abuse you.–Luke 6:28
Bless those who persecute you; bless and do not curse them.–Romans 12:14

Do well to them in practical ways that meet physical needs.

Love your enemies; do good to those who hate you.–Luke 6:27
As you wish that others would do to you, do so to them.–Luke 6:31
See that no one repays anyone evil for evil, but always seek to do good to one another and to everyone.–1 Thessalonians 5:15
If your enemy is hungry, feed him; if he is thirsty, give him something to drink; for by so doing you will heap burning coals on his head.–Romans 12:20

Do not retaliate when personally wronged.

Do not repay evil for evil or reviling for reviling, but on the contrary, bless, for to this you were called, that you may obtain a blessing.–1 Peter 3:9

Repay no one evil for evil…Beloved, never avenge yourselves, but leave it to the wrath of God, for it is written, "Vengeance is mine, I will repay, says the Lord."–Romans 12:17, 19

Live peaceably with them as much as it depends on you.

If possible, so far as it depends on you, live peaceably with all.–Romans 12:18

Pursue their joyful freedom from sin and from condemnation by telling them the truth of Christ.

Jesus said to the Jews who had believed in him, "If you abide in my word, you are truly my disciples, and you will know the truth, and the truth will set you free."–John 8:31-32

Earnestly desire that they join you in heaven with the Father by showing them the way: Jesus Christ.

Brothers, my heart's desire…for them are that they may be saved.–Romans 10:1

Jesus said to him, "I am the way, and the truth, and the life. No one comes to the Father except through me."–John 14:6

"Whoever believes in him shall not perish but have eternal life."–John 3:16

Seek to comprehend the meaning of what they say, so that your affirmations or criticisms are based on true understanding, not distortion or caricature.

Love does not rejoice at wrong, but rejoices with the truth.–1 Corinthians 13:6

Warn them with tears that those who do not receive Jesus Christ as the crucified and risen Savior who takes away the sins of the world will perish under the wrath of God.

But to all who did receive him, who believed in his name, he gave the right to become children of God.–John 1:12

If you confess with your mouth that Jesus is Lord and believe in your heart that God raised him from the dead, you will be saved.–Romans 10:9

For many, of whom I have often told you and now tell you even with tears, walk as enemies of the cross of Christ.–Philippians 3:18

Don't mislead them or give them false hope by saying, "Muslims worship the true God."

This statement communicates to almost everybody a positive picture of the Muslim heart knowing, loving, and honoring the true God. But Jesus makes a person's response to himself the litmus test of the authenticity of a person's response to God. And he is explicit that if a person rejects him as the Divine One who gives his life as a ransom for sins and rises again—that person does not know, love, or honor the true God.

They said to [Jesus] therefore, "Where is your Father?" Jesus answered, "You know neither me nor my Father. If you knew me, you would know my Father also."–John 8:19

Whoever does not honor the Son does not honor the Father who sent him.–John 5:23

[Jesus said,] "I know that you do not have the love of God within you. I have come in my Father's name, and you do not receive me."–John 5:42-43

Love will not mislead Muslims, or those who care about Muslims, by saying that they "know" or "honor" and "love" the true God when they do not receive Jesus for who he really is. We cannot see people's hearts. How do we know if they know and honor and love the true God? We lay down our lives to offer them Jesus. If they receive him, they know and love and honor God. If they don't, they don't. Jesus is the test.

That is the point of Jesus' words in Luke 10:16, "The one who rejects me rejects him who sent me." And in Matthew 10:40, "Whoever receives me receives him who sent me." And in John 5:46, "If you believed Moses, you would believe me."

The most loving thing we can do for Muslims, or anyone else, is to tell them the whole truth about Jesus Christ, in the context of sacrificial care for them and willingness to suffer for them rather than abandon them, and then plead with them to turn away from "vain worship" (Mark 7:7) and receive Christ as the crucified and risen Savior for the forgiveness of their sins and the hope of eternal life. This would be our great joy—to have brothers and sisters from all the Muslim peoples of the world.

Making a decision

Whichever plan you follow, do not leave anyone only with the facts of the gospel and his knowledge of where he stands with God. You need to bring him to the place of decision. His decision may be not to believe and receive Christ as Savior and Lord, but it is a decision nevertheless. Many people are able to share Christ with others, but the problem often comes in getting them to receive the Lord. Disciples must know how to reap—how to lead people across the line, so to speak, of receiving Christ as their Savior.

We have to make sure the person with whom we have shared the gospel understands four basic things.

He must believe that he is a sinner.

He must know that judgment is sure to come and that there is a spiritual penalty of death for sin.

He must believe that Jesus Christ came to this earth and died on the cross for *his* sins.

He must know that he needs to repent of his sins and put his trust and faith in Jesus Christ alone. Ask, "Do these things make sense to you?" At this point you are beginning to change from presenting the facts, to asking the person what he is going to do about the facts he now says he understands.

The final question that should be asked is: "Would you like to receive this gift of eternal life?" If he then says "yes," lead him in a prayer of confession of sin, belief in Jesus Christ, and acceptance of eternal life. If he says "no," then either review the facts or consider the fleetingness of life and what happens when a person does not know Jesus Christ. A true disciple of Jesus Christ must be involved in evangelism. If he isn't, then he is not a disciple but a convert who is still immature in vital areas of Christian discipleship. It is impossible to be a disciple without communicating the gospel to others.

How to share the Gospel without getting into an argument

"Not by might, nor by power, but by my Spirit, says the Lord of Hosts" – Zechariah 4:6

How many times have you wanted to share your faith without getting into an argument? Consider this approach...

Step # 1. Opening Questions
Do you have any kind of belief? To you, who is Jesus? Do you think there is a Heaven or hell? If you fell over and died, where would you go? If heaven, why would God let you in?

By the way, if what you believed was NOT true, would you want to know?

If "Yes"–open your Bible If "No"–do nothing.

How can they argue with you when it's their own opinion that is being stated?

Important note:
When ministering to the Muslim, do not use a Bible where you have written personal notes, or have colored Bible verses. For many of them it can be translated as irreverent to God.

Step # 2. The Reverse!
Ask, "what does Luke 10:25-28 say to you? Open your Bible; turn it toward the other person.

* They will be doing the reading. * They will be doing the talking.
* The Holy Spirit will be doing the convincing.

Who can they argue with ?
They will talk… You will listen. God's Word will bring the conviction.

Here follow some suggested scriptures you can share.

With each Scripture ask: What does this say to you?"

We are separated from God by sin. "For the wages of sin is death, but the free gift of God is eternal life in Christ Jesus."–Rom. 6:23

God's plan of salvation:

"For God so loved the world, that He gave His only begotten Son, that whoever believes in Him should not perish, but have eternal life.–John 3:16

The death of Jesus Christ in our place is God's only provision for man's sin:

"He who was delivered up because of our transgressions, and was raised because of our justification."-Rom. 4:25

We must personally receive Jesus Christ as Savior and Lord:

"But as many as received Him, to them He gave the right to become children of God, even those who believe in His name."–John 1:12.

"For by grace you have been saved through faith; and not of yourselves, it is the gift of God; not as a result of works, that no one should boast."–Eph. 2:8,9

The Choice is ours!
Jesus said; "Here I am standing at the door…"–Jesus–Revelations 3:20

In Closure, step #3 Receiving Christ
Five important questions:
Are you a sinner? Do you want forgiveness of sins? Do you believe Jesus Christ died on the cross for you and rose again? Are you willing to surrender your life to Jesus Christ? Are you ready to invite Jesus Christ into your heart?

How to become a child of God…

Confess your sin to God.

Decide to turn from your sin. (Repent)

Believe that Jesus Christ died in your place on the cross and rose from the grave, to give you eternal life.–Romans. 10:9

Invite Jesus Christ to come into your life as your personal Lord and Savior.

You can receive Christ right now through prayer.

God knows your heart and is not so concerned with your words as He is with the attitude of your heart.

Following is a suggested prayer:

Dear Father, I am a sinner who needs Jesus to be the Lord of my life. I want to turn from sin. Please forgive me my sin and come into my life. Please help me, and teach me to become that person you want me to be. I believe that Jesus died for my sins, and that those who believe shall be saved. Thank you Father, for giving me hope, and forgiveness of my sin. In Jesus name, Amen.

After you lead them in accepting and submitting to Christ, assure them that God has met them and done something extremely exciting in them. Remind them of their commitment and help them with their new life in Christ by sharing these ways to deepen this new relationship:

Read your Bible every day to hear God's word to you.

Talk to God in prayer everyday.

Tell others about Jesus Christ.

Go to a Bible-believing church, to experience fellowship with other believers and worship God.

Get baptized in water. Acts 2:38 reads, "Repent and be baptized, every one of you, in the name of Jesus Christ for the forgiveness of your sins, and you will receive the gift of the Holy Spirit. This promise is for you and your children, and for all who are far off, for all whom the Lord our God will call."

Demonstrate your new life by your love and concern for others as you are Christ's representative in a needy world.

Ways to handle, and not handle the Gospel:

Don't be ashamed of it

"I am not ashamed of the gospel, because it is the power of God for the salvation of everyone who believes: first for the Jew, then for the Gentile. For in the gospel righteousness from God is revealed, a righteousness that is by faith from first to last, just as it is written: 'The righteous will live by faith.'"–Rom. 1:16-17;

Don't pervert it.

"I am astonished that you are so quickly deserting the one who called you by the grace of Christ and are turning to a different gospel—which is really no gospel at all. Evidently some people are throwing you into confusion and are trying to pervert the gospel of Christ. But even if we or an angel from heaven should preach a gospel other than the one we preached to you, let him be eternally condemned! As we have already said, so now I say again: If anybody is preaching to you a gospel other than what you accepted, let him be eternally condemned!" Gal. 1:6-9

"For it is by grace you have been saved, through faith—and this not from yourselves, it is the gift of God..."–Eph. 2:8

"I warn everyone who hears the words of the prophecy of this book: If anyone adds anything to them, God will add to him the plagues described in this book. And if anyone takes words away from this book of prophecy, God will take away from him his share in the tree of life and in the holy city, which are described in this book."–Rev. 22:19-20

Obey it.

"Do not merely listen to the word, and so deceive yourselves. Do what it says. Anyone who
listens to the word but does not do what it says is like a man who looks

at his face in a mirror and, after looking at himself, goes away and immediately forgets what he looks like. But the man who looks intently into the perfect law that gives freedom, and continues to do this, not forgetting what he has heard, but doing it—he will be blessed in what he does."–James 1:22-25

"As the body without the spirit is dead, so faith without deeds is dead."–James 2:26

Defend it.

Paul did, he wrote: *"I thank my God every time I remember you. In all my prayers for all of you, I always pray with joy because of your partnership in the gospel from the first day until now, being confident of this, that he who began a good work in you will carry it on to completion until the day of Christ Jesus. It is right for me to feel this way about all of you, since I have you in my heart; for whether I am in chains or defending and confirming the gospel, all of you share in God's grace with me."–Phil. 1:3-7*

"What you heard from me, keep as the pattern of sound teaching, with faith and love in Christ Jesus. Guard the good deposit that was entrusted to you—guard it with the help of the Holy Spirit who lives in us."–2 Tim. 1: 13,14

Hold fast to it.

"Now, brothers, I want to remind you of the gospel I preached to you, which you received and on which you have taken your stand. By this gospel you are saved, if you hold firmly to the word I preached to you. Otherwise, you have believed in vain."–1 Corinthians 15:1-2

Love it.

* Thinking about the greatest command:
Love the Lord your God with all your heart and with all your soul and with all your strength and with all your mind'; and, 'Love your neighbor as yourself.' "–Luke 10:27

Remember, John 1 tells us that the Jesus is the Word, thus I do not believe that you can love God, without loving His Word.

'Whatever happens, conduct yourselves in a manner worthy of the gospel of Christ. Then, whether I come and see you or only hear about you in my absence, I will know that you stand firm in one spirit, contending as one man for the faith of the gospel."–Phil 1:27;

Preach it.

Jesus said to them, *"Go into all the world and preach the good news to all creation. Whoever believes and is baptized will be saved, but whoever does not believe will be condemned."–Mark 16:15-16*

"I am obligated both to Greeks and non-Greeks, both to the wise and the foolish. That is why I am so eager to preach the gospel also to you who are at Rome. I am not ashamed of the gospel, because it is the power of God for the salvation of everyone who believes: first for the Jew, then for the Gentile. For in the gospel a righteousness from God is revealed, a righteousness that is by faith from first to last, just as it is written: 'The righteous will live by faith.'"–Rom. 1:15-16

"Yet when I preach the gospel, I cannot boast, for I am compelled to preach. Woe to me if I do not preach the gospel! If I preach voluntarily, I have a reward; if not voluntarily, I am simply discharging the trust committed to me."–1 Cor. 9:16, 17

Samuel said, "As for me, far be it from me that I should sin against the LORD by failing to pray for you. And I will teach you the way that is good and right."–1 Sam. 12:23

Remember always: The Gospel was not given to be hoarded, but to be shared!

Trust in it.

"My son, do not forget my teaching, but keep my commands in your

heart, for they will prolong your life many years and bring you prosperity. Let love and faithfulness never leave you; bind them around your neck, write them on the tablet of your heart. Then you will win favor and a good name in the sight of God and man. Trust in the LORD with all your heart and lean not on your own understanding; in all your ways acknowledge him, and he will make your paths straight."–Proverbs 3:1-6.

"Therefore everyone who hears these words of mine and puts them into practice is like a wise man who built his house on the rock. The rain came down, the streams rose, and the winds blew and beat against that house; yet it did not fall, because it had its foundation on the rock. But everyone who hears these words of mine and does not put them into practice is like a foolish man who built his house on sand. The rain came down, the streams rose, and the winds blew and beat against that house, and it fell with a great crash."–Matt. 7:24-27

"Reflect on what I am saying, for the Lord will give you insight into all this. Remember Jesus Christ, raised from the dead, descended from David. This is my gospel, for which I am suffering even to the point of being chained like a criminal. But God's word is not chained. Therefore I endure everything for the sake of the elect that they too may obtain the salvation that is in Christ Jesus, with eternal glory. Here is a trustworthy saying: If we died with him, we will also live with him; if we endure, we will also reign with him. If we disown him, he will also disown us; if we are faithless, he will remain faithful, for he cannot disown himself."–2 Tim 2:7-13

"This is what the LORD says: 'Cursed is the one who trusts in man, who depends on flesh for his strength and whose heart turns away from the LORD. He will be like a bush in the wastelands; he will not see prosperity when it comes. He will dwell in the parched places of the desert, in a salt land where no one lives. But blessed is the man who trusts in the LORD, whose confidence is in him. He will be like a tree planted by the water that sends out its roots by the stream. It does not fear when heat comes; its leaves are always green. It has no worries in a year of drought and never fails to bear fruit' The heart is deceitful above all things and beyond cure.

Who can understand it? 'I the LORD search the heart and examine the mind, to reward a man according to his conduct, according to what his deeds deserve.'"–Jeremiah 17:5-10

6. "Unconditional Surrender"

"Submit yourselves, then, to God. Resist the devil, and he will flee from you. Come near to God and he will come near to you. Wash your hands, you sinners, and purify your hearts, you double-minded. Grieve, mourn and wail. Change your laughter to mourning and your joy to gloom. Humble yourselves before the Lord, and he will lift you up."–James 4:7-10

As you have read my story you know that after I met God I was not the same person I was before my cry for help. I had gotten saved, filled with the Holy Spirit, and become very active in sharing my story with those around me; so had you met me on the streets of my hometown after my big return from the sea you might have barely recognized me. On the surface, dramatic events like these would seem to be all I needed to finally get my life in order, but underneath I was still very much out of control.

It is not that when you get saved, you pull a switch and all the bad leaves, and the good just shows up with Fed-Ex over night delivery. Prior to my desperate cry for help, I had grown as a survivalist, an independent. Sailors are rough people, and I had become someone who had learned to stand up for himself. I carried a big knife on my waist, and anyone who wanted trouble, just had to eye my hand reaching for my belt. One look and they would see where I got my protection from. I had a big mouth and talked a lot of bluff. Though I might have turned that one page by getting saved and leaving the ship, my life was still very much unchecked. I was still kind of like a wild horse, which had been caught but was not yet broken. Nothing could bridle me. God saw how I needed to be harnessed, so that I could be more useful for his kingdom, and ultimately he had a plan. I needed to learn to trust in God and people. After being guarded for so long; I had to learn not to be in control. I had to learn to be led, and not just do my own thing. What's more, I needed to get healed from all the emotional scars I had collected throughout the years.

The interesting thing that many have a tendency to forget: we might run away from our hurts, trouble and disappointments, we can escape the location and the circumstances from which the scars came from, but wounds and scars themselves, you will take with you until they are they are laid at the feet of Christ. Such scars had left unhealthy imprints behind, and until I was going to let Jesus heal me, I was allowing them to hinder me in my spiritual walk. What was worse, I was carrying around greater potential to hurt others too. For it happens so often that when you grow up in an un-healthy atmosphere: you're odds "jab skyward" that you will copy what you have experienced, doing the same to others in your later years.

When I had left the ship, going back to the place were I grew up, I had no idea what I was going to do next, but it seems that God did. In the early 70's my country was still drafting young men to go to the military. Not long after coming home there was a letter in the mailbox, addressed to my name from the ministry of defense. I needed to come and do my physical, and then I would find out were I was going to serve. Having worked on board of a ship the last couple of years, I assumed that they would put me in the navy, for that would make sense. However when I had completed my physical, they told me that I was placed in the army. Later, I was ordered to boot camp, and the harnessing began. Learning the drills, marching, running in full gear, getting up so early that you could still see the stars, being in your bunk by curfew…From making your bed, to folding clothes and polishing your shoes, everything was to bring me under control to a higher standard. You might understand that these were all things I really did not care for doing, but when I wanted to stay out of trouble I had to submit to the authorities above me. Being in that place of instruction taught me to discipline myself, and brought a little order to the chaos of my existence. I also started to meet other Christians who were from the same town I came from, and had the heart to follow after God. Another few pieces to the puzzle of my life were being fitted into place, and many others have followed since.

Placed under God's authority

A disciple puts Jesus Christ first in all areas of his life. He is making Jesus its center. It is not calling Jesus to be Lord, but making Him Lord!

Doing a word study on the word "submission" found in James 4:7, we learn that it means to put yourself under God, under His care, power and strength; to yield to God, to His Will, command, instructions, laws behavior and Word; to surrender yourself to God for Him to strengthen you so you can do exactly what He says. It is a complete yielding to the "Hands of the Potter."

The acknowledgment of Jesus Christ being Lord is the taking of the "I" from the throne of our life and place Jesus in that place.

Jesus Christ being Lord in a believer's life is the most crucial issue in Christian living. All of our aspirations, the blessings, and joys of the Christian life are absolutely dependent on our submission to Him as Lord of our life. We cannot experience the fullest in Christian living until we commit ourselves unconditionally to the lordship of Christ.

Furthermore, submission to Christ's lordship is not a one-time experience. We must make Jesus Christ Lord of our life on a daily, moment by moment basis and in every decision we make. It is absolutely necessary and the foundation of Christian discipleship.

God said, *"'I AM WHO I AM'... 'I AM has sent me to you'"*–Exodus 3:14

The Bible uses many different words and concepts to describe God; these are not just theological terms but facts about God that vitally concern all of us. In order to acknowledge him as Lord practically, we have to know what he is like.

The One True God

The one true God has revealed Himself as the eternally self-existent "I AM," the Creator of heaven and earth and the Redeemer of mankind. He has further revealed Himself as embodying the principles of relationship and association as Father Son and Holy Spirit.

"Hear, O Israel: The Lord our God, the Lord is one!–Deuteronomy 6:4

Scripture tells us that God is eternal, all-powerful, all-knowing, always present, great, majestic, glorious and more.

"You are my witnesses," declares the LORD, "and my servant whom I have chosen, so that you may know and believe me and understand that I am he. Before me no god was formed, nor will there be one after me. I, even I, am the LORD, and apart from me there is no savior. I have revealed and saved and proclaimed—I, and not some foreign god among you. You are my witnesses," declares the LORD, "that I am God. Yes, and from ancient days I am he. No one can deliver out of my hand. When I act, who can reverse it?" This is what the LORD says—your Redeemer, the Holy One of Israel: "For your sake I will send to Babylon and bring down as fugitives all the Babylonians, in the ships in which they took pride. I am the LORD, your Holy One, Israel's Creator, your King."–Isaiah 43:10-15

After a life of serving God, King David cried out: "Yours, O Lord, is the greatness and the power and the glory and the majesty and the splendor, for everything in heaven and earth is yours. Yours, O Lord, is the kingdom; you are exalted as head over all. Wealth and honor come from you; you are the ruler of all things. In your hands are strength and power to exalt and give strength to all. Now, our God, we give you thanks, and praise your glorious name." (1 Chronicles 29:11-13)

Jesus said, "I tell you the truth, I am the gate for the sheep. All who ever came before me were thieves and robbers, but the sheep did not listen to them. I am the gate; whoever enters through me will be saved. He will come in and go out, and find pasture. The thief comes only to steal and kill and destroy; I have come that they may have life, and have it to the full. "I am the good shepherd. The good shepherd lays down his life for the sheep.–John 10:7-12

Not only is Jesus Christ Lord because he is God, but he is also Lord by virtue of the salvation that he secured for us. We can never save ourselves. He alone has provided the redemption necessary for us to have eternal life with him. And because he has, he must be Lord of all.

Jesus as the Lamb of God being worshiped by the uncountable hosts of heaven:

Then I looked and heard the voice of many angels, numbering thousands upon thousands, and ten thousand times ten thousand. They encircled the throne and the living creatures and the elders. In a loud voice they sang: 'Worthy is the Lamb, who was slain, to receive power and wealth and wisdom and strength and honor and glory and praise. (Revelation 5:11-12).

"So he became as much superior to the angels as the name he has inherited is superior to theirs" (Hebrews 1:4). We see this clearly in the Old Testament where God the Father, God the Son, and God the Holy Spirit (the Trinity), is worshiped by the angels, or seraphs. They cry out, *"Holy, holy, holy is the Lord Almighty"–Isaiah 6:1-4.*

"And having disarmed the powers and authorities, He (JESUS) *made a public spectacle of them, triumphing over them by the cross"– Colossians 2:15.*

Jesus Christ is the absolute victor over sin, death, hell, and Satan. Through Jesus we can be victorious over every temptation: *"No temptation has seized you except what is common to man. And God is faithful; he will not let you be tempted beyond what you can bear. But when you are tempted, he will also provide a way out so that you can stand up under it"–1 Corinthians 10:13.*

Paul states, *"If God is for us, who can be against us? No, in all these things we are more than conquerors through him who loved us"–Romans 8:31, 37.*

Paul wrote: *"Everyone has heard about your obedience, so I am full of joy over you; but I want you to be wise about what is good, and innocent about what is evil. The God of peace will soon crush Satan under your feet. The grace of our Lord Jesus be with you." –Romans 16:19-20*

The whole world is in the palm of His Hand

Pharaoh discovered this when he tried to keep God's people slaves in Egypt. God told him, *"But I have raised you up for this very purpose, that*

I might show you my power and that my name might be proclaimed in all the earth"–Exodus 9:16.

The king of Babylon, Nebuchadnezzar, declared, *"All the peoples of the earth are regarded as nothing. He does as he pleases with the powers of heaven and the peoples of the earth. No one can hold back his hand or say to him: 'What have you done?'"–Daniel 4:35*

The final authorities over the world we live in do not reside in Europe, the USA, Asia or even in the Middle East. The final authority is in the hands of God and in the hands of his Christ. He is the Lord over the nations of the world.

Jesus is the image of the invisible God, the firstborn over all creation. For by him all things were created: things in heaven and on earth, visible and invisible, whether thrones or powers or rulers or authorities; all things were created by him and for him. He is before all things, and in him all things hold together.–Colossians 1:15-17.

Everything visible and invisible was created by Jesus Christ and is sustained by him. In one shovelful of dirt are thousands of forms of life, all created by Jesus Christ. Beyond our earth are millions of galaxies and stars. All of these were made by Jesus Christ. We cannot even begin to fathom inner space with its atoms, electrons, protons, and neutrons that are all whirling around at tremendous rates of speed, but the Bible says that Jesus Christ made them all. Everything made is subject to the lordship of Christ.

Place your self under God's authority

Christians may acknowledge Jesus as Savior and Lord with their lips but their heart is uncommitted toward Him. However, when Christians do not acknowledge Christ's authority, they leave behind ruined lives of mediocrity and uselessness.

We have countless examples of God's anger with Christians who do not submit to Christ's lordship. The prophetic books of the Old Testament (Isaiah—Malachi) show God's anger toward his people because they did not respond to his lordship. If God were not angry with man's rebellion, he would not be consistent with his holiness, righteousness, and justice. Paul declared, *"For we must all appear before the judgment seat of Christ, that each one may receive what is due him for the things done while in the body, whether good or bad"–2 Corinthians 5:10*. His judgment will be affected by whether or not we have submitted to the lordship of Christ.

What is His plan for us?

"...I have come that they may have life, and have it to the full."–Jesus (John 10:10)

It is when we submit ourselves to God, His word, His will, and His Way for our life's that we will realize his plan and purpose for our life. That is why Scripture says:

"For I know the plans I have for you," declares the LORD, "plans to prosper you and not to harm you, plans to give you hope and a future. Then you will call upon me and come and pray to me, and I will listen to you. You will seek me and find me when you seek me with all your heart. I will be found by you," declares the LORD, "and will bring you back from captivity...".–Jeremiah 29:11-14a

It was during one of my devotions, while I was praying for God's direction and provision for our ministry that the Holy Spirit spoke to my heart. He said that he wanted me to become a shepherd. To be completely honest with you, I had absolutely no desire to be a shepherd, and to add to this argument, I had no clue on how to be one either. But like several times before, The Holy Spirit gently repeated Himself to me with those same words, "I want you to become a shepherd." So finally giving in, I said, "ok" Lord, but you better teach me how to become one.

Now a week or so before this, we had received a letter in the mail from the "Youth With A Mission" base in Amsterdam, This was the same ministry we were involved with before we came to the United States. In their letter they were inviting us to join them in one of their "Go" teams. This was a two week evangelistic mission outreach throughout Europe. My wife and I were very excited about this, and we would love to join them in this adventure. Having to raise money to be able to go on this mission's trip, we prayed for God's provision, we wrote news letters, we told the pastor and the people of our church, hoping that they would like to support us prayerfully and financially.

It was about the second Sunday after God's speaking to me about me becoming a shepherd. We were still raising money for our mission trip, that while we were at church we were approached by an elderly couple. They told us that while they were praying, God spoke to their hearts, and said that they should give us some of their sheep and their lambs.

Being excited about this gift, we accepted them gratefully, and without really thinking about it, I brought them directly to the auction with intending to sell them right away, so we would have the money for our mission's trip. However we discovered quickly that the price of sheep and lamb was very low at that time, and the money we gained from them was not enough to help us on our way.

What happened next shows God's persistence. It was a couple of day's later that we received a visit from one of our neighbors who lived about five miles down the road from us. He was a farmer and he had seen us at the auction selling our sheep, and was wondering if we would be interested in raising bummer lambs. These are newborn lambs that have been rejected by their mother, and would die unless someone would bottle feed them until they would be strong enough to take care of them selves. He said he had several of those lambs but had no time to take care of them himself, and was willing to give them to us when we were interested. Me, still thinking about all the money we needed to raise for our mission's trip thought that this could be just what we needed.

After accepting the neighbors offer, we ended up raising bummer lambs, sometimes four to six at the time. It did not take long that I learned that raising lambs required much more then just turning milk powder into milk, and putting a bottle into their mouths. Some of the lambs were eager to drink, however there were others who rejected the bottle and choose to die rather then to eat the food they so desperately needed.

Of course you can understand that when you put a lot of effort into these cute little animals, having to fight for their lives in some cases—doing about anything humanly possible to save them; it breaks your heart when some of them died never the less.

My wife and I ended up raising bummer lambs for about two seasons, and had in spite of all our losses a lot of fun doing it.

The interesting part of this story is, that after all our effort in raising lambs; we never made it to go on the planned mission trip; however God gave us a lot of teachings about being a shepherd. It was about two years later that I got ordained by the leadership of our Church, and not long after that we received an invitation to come, and join Teen Challenge…being a shepherd, shepherding people with life controlling problems.

Submitting our selves to God

This submission does not mean that He wants to keep us under His thumb, but that we mite place our selves under His protective wings while aligning ourselves to:

His Word–Our ultimate authority (John 14:6, Rev. 19:13);
His will—Being obedient His Word and His leading (John 7:16-18);
His way—We need to follow His blueprint. Just as Moses was building the tabernacle—Exodus 26…); or, Noah has build the ark–Gen. 6:13-22).

Out of my personal experience I learned that it is not difficult to assume that we have all the talents, abilities, and experiences we need to do well. But the truth is, we are better off, to remember to always remain humble in our Christian walk, and to take heed to the Words of God found in Isaiah 55:8: *"For my thoughts are not your thoughts, neither are your ways my ways," declares the LORD…"*

Just think of it, we can say that we are born again Christians, but when we are still copying what everybody else is doing for the sake of acceptance, or following our own ideas, desires and opinions, or we are persisting on doing things our own way rather then God's, we could still be walking in an attitude of rebellion. (Proverbs 16:2; 1 Thessalonians. 2:4b)

Submission at All Times in Every Area of Our Life

God's plan for us is to be like Jesus Christ. When we read about his life, we realize that he was totally submissive to the father. Jesus said that his whole purpose in life was *"to do the will of him who sent me and to finish his work"–John 4:34.*

If we are to be like Jesus Christ, then we must be submissive to him at all times. *"For those God foreknew he also predestined to be conformed to the likeness of his Son"–Romans 8:29.*

None of us can stand before God and say that we have always done things that please him. Our problem is centered in the heart where our self-will still struggles with the lordship decision. It is more often easier for us to do something that is not in the will of God than to do his will. But God has promised us the power to overcome self and to be submissive to his lordship (Romans 6). Since his plan is for us to become like Jesus, he will help us reach this goal.

Submitting to God in our life is a constant struggle for most of us.

While ministering at Teen Challenge much of our counseling had to do with submission to God and His Word.

If only people would submit to God, then a particular problem area could be settled. But people do not want to submit to the authority of God, so the problems persist.

Be self-controlled and alert. Your enemy the devil prowls around like a roaring lion looking for someone to devour. Resist him, standing firm in the faith, because you know that your brothers throughout the world are undergoing the same kind of sufferings.–1 Peter 5:8,9

When we make the decision to yield to the lordship of Jesus Christ, our flesh will immediately lead us in a spiritual battle.

Let me give you some personal examples:

We tend to look at life from our point of view rather than God's point of view.

"For my thoughts are not your thoughts, neither are your ways my

ways," declares the Lord. "As the heavens are higher than the earth, so are my ways higher than your ways and my thoughts than your thoughts.– Isaiah 55:8-9

Somehow we do not recognize that God always wants the best for us. Yet he who knows the end from the beginning knows what's best for us far better than we do. As you look back on your life, are there some things you might want to change? There probably are many. But would you want to change anything in which you had clearly done the will of God? I doubt it. You knew that you were doing what was best for you.

God may ask us to do something we don't want to do, or give up something we're not willing to give up.

* To many people this is a real barrier to a lordship decision. He may ask us to spend time with someone we would rather not be a friend to.
* He may ask us to move to another part of the country, to live in a foreign country,
* Give our "price possession" away, or have somebody else play with your "toys."

Yes, sometimes God will take away what we like keep. In these cases, we can be sure that it would eventually be wrong for us or possibly destroy our spiritual life and ministry. When we trust Jesus Christ as Savior, we will completely turn over our eternal futures to him. We do that because we believe that he knows what is best for us.

This requires surrender, an actual release to God. Here is where we have a real test of faith, for it takes faith to completely surrender anything we cherish to God.

So many of us accept God's offer of salvation by grace through faith, but insist on keeping the steering wheel in our own hands, while missing out on the ride of their spiritual life.

Obedience is tied into a lordship decision.

You cannot separate obedience and submission, or disobedience from rebellion.

Let's look at four stages of disobedience. It could be good thing to evaluate our life in light of them periodically.

"I am going to do what I want to do no matter what God wants."
Many Christians realize that this is wrong, but they still live according to this pattern. Essentially they do not want Christ to rule their life.

"If God will give me what I want first, then I will give him an equal exchange.
"This is bargaining with God; I will give him what *I* think is an equal exchange. If God will only give me the job that I want, then I will give him some of my time in exchange.

"If God will give me what I want first, then I will give him what he wants."
This is also bargaining with God. This stage is similar to the second stage, but includes a willingness to give God what he wants.

"I will give God what he wants first, and then in faith believe that he will give me what I want."
This has finally reversed the "me-first" approach, but it is still a form of bargaining. I am expecting God to do something for me because I have done something for him.

Obedience and submission say's: "I will give God whatever he wants, regardless of whether he gives me what I want." This is lordship in practice. This is the crucial stage in our obedience.
Being on board of the ship, desperate for help, God did not just meet my needs for that moment, He asked me to leave my future in His hand. I needed to let go of being in control. It was when I left the ship that I started to become the person He wanted for me to be.
Practicing Christ's lordship is the first real step of becoming a disciple of the Lord Jesus Christ, and it is the most vital one.

I encourage you to evaluate your life and be sure that you are totally submitted to the lordship of Jesus Christ. You can know the fullness of

Christian living only when Jesus Christ is Lord and the center of your life. It is the way God has ordained for us to live from the beginning of time.

As for you, you were dead in your transgressions and sins, in which you used to live when you followed the ways of this world and of the ruler of the kingdom of the air, the spirit who is now at work in those who are disobedient. All of us also lived among them at one time, gratifying the cravings of our sinful nature and following its desires and thoughts. Like the rest, we were by nature objects of wrath. But because of his great love for us, God, who is rich in mercy, made us alive with Christ even when we were dead in transgressions—it is by grace you have been saved. And God raised us up with Christ and seated us with him in the heavenly realms in Christ Jesus, in order that in the coming ages he might show the incomparable riches of his grace, expressed in his kindness to us in Christ Jesus. For it is by grace you have been saved, through faith—and this not from yourselves, it is the gift of God–not by works, so that no one can boast. For we are God's workmanship, created in Christ Jesus to do good works, which God prepared in advance for us to do.–Ephesians 2:1-10

7. Continuing Steadfastly

Those who accepted his message were baptized, and about three thousand were added to their number that day. They devoted themselves to the apostles' teaching and to the fellowship, to the breaking of bread and to prayer. Everyone was filled with awe, and many wonders and miraculous signs were done by the apostles. All the believers were together and had everything in common. Selling their possessions and goods, they gave to anyone as he had need. Every day they continued to meet together in the temple courts. They broke bread in their homes and ate together with glad and sincere hearts, praising God and enjoying the favor of all the people. And the Lord added to their number daily those who were being saved.–Acts 2:41-47

As I was once a wandering sheep, disconnected from a healthy place were I could spiritually grow, I needed to find a place were I felt I fitted in. First coming back in my home town, I went back to the church I came from. I started to help in Sunday school for little children, and even though that was fun, I still did not feel to be at the right place. Somehow I felt confused, God had genuinely saved me, given me a revelation of His power and a new vision, but somehow this church seemed to stand still. Even when I shared my story, and was excited about the things of God, I felt looked upon as if I was still rebellious, weird, too radical and out of place. I still felt labeled and pushed in a box.

It was when I met people who had similar salvation experiences that God lead me to a place of worship that I could call my home. It was at that place that I became aware that I never made my own decision to get baptized in water as an act of obedience to God (Acts 2:38). It was the place where I learned Biblical truths, about having a personal relationship with Jesus. It was a place that encouraged me to become an active participant in the services, a place where I could build friendship relationships, and continue in fulfilling the Great Commission. And it was a place where people loved and accepted me just as I was.

A disciple attends church regularly to worship God, to make a contribution to the body of believers, and to have his spiritual needs met.

If we trace the history of the church since the time of Christ, we find periods of unrest, falling away, and corruption. Yet God has always had a faithful remnant of disciples throughout the centuries. Today, as hundreds of years ago, the Scriptures call all Christ's disciples to be men and women to be involved in the church and to be active participants in fulfilling the great Commission. This is reaching the world with the gospel.

The first mention of the church in the New Testament was when Jesus asked his disciples who they thought he was. Peter made a great profession of faith. *"You are the Christ, the Son of the living God." Jesus replied, "Blessed are you, Simon son of Jonah, for this was not revealed to you by man, but by my Father in heaven. And I tell you that you are Peter, and on this rock I will build my church, and the gates of Hades will not overcome it"–Matthew 16:16-18.*

The central thrust of the Great Commission is the making of disciples. It is a continuous process in which men and women are converted to Jesus Christ, brought into a living fellowship or body of responsible believers, and in time become reproductive Christians. This is the main task of the church today, a task in which every disciple must find his place.

The New Testament church

The people of God are one throughout all ages, being those who believe God. They anticipated the Messiah in the Old Testament and trusted Jesus as Savior and Lord in the New. But the New Testament church is uniquely Jesus', for he is the one who formed it and has been building it on confessions similar to Peter's. Between the resurrection and ascension of Jesus, there were over 500 believers in the Lord (1 Corinthians 15:6). These were men and women who were fully committed to the evangelistic task and were in absolute obedience to the Lord's command. He had told them to wait for the coming of the Holy Spirit, who was to give them the power to do what they had been commanded to do. The promised Holy Spirit came on them on the Day of Pentecost (see Acts 2).

The waiting disciples were filled with the Holy Spirit and were enabled to speak in the languages of the many visitors in Jerusalem. Immediately they began to witness, and they were heard and understood by Jewish people from many nations of the Mediterranean and Near East. Their communication was so effective that it resulted in 3,000 professions of faith. These new believers were then baptized, identifying themselves with the church, and were added to the fellowship of those already believing. As soon as the new converts were incorporated into the church, their training in Christian living began. Luke records for us what happened to accomplish that training.

> They were instructed by the leadership of the church.
> They participated in the fellowship of the church.
> They joined with other believers in communion.
> They learned how to pray and devoted themselves to it.
> They observed the apostles as they preached and performed miracles.
> They realized their responsibility to one another in material things and had everything in common.
> They were generous in their sharing with those in need.
> They met together daily for worship in the temple.
> They gathered together in homes and ate with one another.
> They worshiped God with praise for what he had done for them.
> They had a good testimony in the city.
> They witnessed God's power as he added to their number daily (see Acts 2:42-47).

In time the new converts became witnesses and joined the mission of the church—carrying out the Great Commission by reproducing the whole process of making disciples.

Thus evangelism in the New Testament does not stop with reaching people with the gospel, nor with the proclamation of the gospel, nor with public professions of faith in the gospel, nor even with relating them to the church through baptism and teaching.

The goal is that these new converts become reproducing Christians who complete the cycle and guarantee the continuous process of evangelism and discipleship.

History tells us that within a single generation, the church of Jesus Christ had penetrated into all parts of the Roman Empire. The gospel was being preached, people were finding Christ as their Savior and Lord, and local churches were established. In the years that followed, the church grew even more rapidly in Roman society. We see some evidence of this growth in the writings of the Apostle Paul. *"We always thank God, the Father of our Lord Jesus Christ, when we pray for you, because we have heard of your faith in Christ Jesus and of the love you have for all the saints—the faith and love that spring from the hope that is stored up for you in heaven and that you have already heard about in the word of truth, the gospel that has come to you. All over the world this gospel is producing fruit and growing, just as it has been doing among you since the day you heard it and understood God's grace in all its truth."* (Colossians 1:3-6)

Historians tell us that by A.D. 323 approximately 10 percent of the Roman Empire's population, some 10 million out of about 100 million, had been won to the new faith. The gospel had also spread beyond the bounds of the empire into the Tigris and Euphrates valleys, along the shores of the Black Sea, into Armenia and Arabia, and even into India. One of the Churches in South India traces its roots all the way back to the Apostle Thomas, one of the Twelve.

God was founding his church in the world. His people, having been filled and empowered by the Spirit of God, were following through with their commitment to Jesus Christ. We can see here, as Jesus had predicted, that "on this rock I will build my church, and the gates of Hades will not overcome it" (Matthew 16:18).

When we study church history, we learn that throughout the years the church struggled through many persecutions, each of which ended with a period of peace before another outbreak came upon it. Not only did the church encounter difficulties from outside in the persecutions of the Roman government, but there were also constant struggles with false teaching and false doctrines. Peter had warned the church of this (see 2 Peter 2), but they arose nevertheless and the church at times succumbed to them. Throughout the centuries this internal attack has continued, and does so to the present day. Multitudes today are being drawn away by modern versions of ancient heresies. Yet there has always been a nucleus of people who have concentrated on the process of making disciples and trying to be obedient to the Great Commission. Many of those who were reached with the gospel message were discipled by godly men and women. Following their conversion some were ostracized and others were martyred for their faith. But the good news continued to spread during that time. With the dawning of the Reformation in the early 16th century, the Holy Spirit moved in the lives of men such as Martin Luther, John Calvin, Jacob Arminius, Moody and others. God used them to bring the Scriptures to the forefront again. Luther and other men translated the Bible into the language of the people and enabled them to read the word of God in their own languages. This return to the Scriptures gave rise to the modern missionary movement, as people, having been challenged by Christ's commission, were moved by the Holy Spirit to commit their lives to Christian service.

Church Leadership

Since God established his church to proclaim salvation, the leadership of the church is his responsibility. He must raise up men who will take the leadership positions in the church. Yet, as with many other biblical doctrines, the church too has a share in the responsibility to raise up leadership within itself that will serve and lead the church for years to come.

The Bible tells us that we are to submit to those in positions of leadership as unto the Lord. The writer to the Hebrews declared: *"Obey your leaders and submit to their authority. They keep watch over you as men who must give an account. Obey them so that their work will be a joy, not a burden, for that would be of no advantage to you"–Hebrews 13:17*. God has placed over us men who are responsible to keep us in the center of the will of God. They are responsible to rebuke us, to restrain us from sin, to restore us to fellowship, and to help us avoid false doctrines and teachings.

Because of the service of leaders in the church, we are to hold them in high respect. Paul wrote: *"Now we ask you, brothers, to respect those who work hard among you, who are over you in the Lord and who admonish you. Hold them in the highest regard in love because of their work"–1 Thessalonians 5:12-13.*

Our responsibility is to respect the leaders of the church whom God has placed over us. Additional teaching on leadership is given to us by Paul. He wrote to the Ephesians: *It was he who gave some to be apostles, some to be prophets, some to be evangelists, and some to be pastors and teachers, to prepare God's people for works of service, so that the body of Christ may be built up until we all reach unity in the faith and in the knowledge of the Son of God and become mature, attaining to the whole measure of the fullness of Christ (Ephesians 4:11-13).*

Some leaders can be recognized as apostles. These are men are given the responsibility of carrying out the Great Commission. They could be involved in planting churches and start new ministries.

Another type of leadership is that of prophet. The New Testament prophet is not one who foretells the future, but rather one who tells forth the word of God. His responsibility is to communicate the word of God and make sure that the people understand it.

Another type of leader is the evangelist. This is a person who has been anointed by God with the special responsibility of communicating the message of the gospel to many people. Just think about evangelist Billy Graham, who has been used of God around the world in leading many people to the Savior through his preaching.

Other leaders in the local church are the pastor, the teachers, the elders and the deacons who shepherd, teach and minister to the needs of the people. These are men who have taken the responsibility of nurturing and ministering to a local congregation.

Many of us have had the privilege in our local churches of sitting at the feet of men of God who have taught us many things and prepared us for our own ministry of leadership.

New Testament qualifications for a spiritual leader.

Above reproach *(Read: Acts 6:3; 1 Timothy 3:2-13; Titus 1:6,7; Acts 6:3)*

The emphasis here is on man's reputation. How he is regarded by those who personal know him. The believers in Lystra reported to Paul that Timothy "was well spoken of by the brethren who were in Lystra and Iconium "(Acts 16:2) A spiritual leader must have a good reputation. Having a positive impact, doing God's work will demand it.

Husband of one wife (*1 Timothy 3:2*)
The Roman culture of Paul's day was accented with moral looseness, much like we have today. Paul concludes that a man must be married to only ONE woman—not divorced—and we might add, living with her in peace, tranquility and fulfillment.

Temperate—[KJV= vigilant] (*1 Timothy 3:2*)
The Greek word behind this qualification for spiritual leaders means "free from excess passion, ruckus, confusion, etc…well balanced, self controlled and watchful." A spiritual leader is well-oriented mentally, spiritually and physically. The spiritual leader must be vigilant, watch over, and control his own life and the lives of his dear people

Sober minded [NASB = Prudent](*1 Timothy 3:2; Titus 1:8)[Greek = Sophrona]*
This word means: Self-controlled; sober; prudent; to live wisely; to be sensible; to have a mind that is sound; controlled, disciplined, chaste, sober—a mind that has complete control over all sensual desire. (When the mind is controlled, a person's whole life–his body and behavior—is controlled. He lives wisely)

Respectable (*1 Timothy 3:2*)
The Holy Spirit is very practical. Here he inspires Paul to speak of the importance of living a well-ordered life. The Greek word is "Kosmion," in its root form, it means to "Put order…adorn, decorate." The spiritual leader is a person who has good conduct, whose character and behavior stand as the ideal and pattern for others.

In *1 Timothy 3:8,* addressing the deacons, the Greek word is "Semnos." Meaning worthy of respect, grave, dignity, highly respected, serious, honorable, reverent and noble.

(This does not mean that the deacon is to walk around with a long face, never smiling, joking, or having fun. It simply means that he is to be serious-minded and committed to Christ and to the mission of the church: the mission of reaching the lost and meeting the desperate needs of the world.)

Hospitable (*1 Timothy 3:2, Titus 1:8*)
A spiritual leader views hospitality not just as asocial grace, but as a way of bringing others into an atmosphere of love and Christian concern.

Able to teach (*1 Timothy 3:2, Titus 1:9*)
The word translated by this phrase "able to teach" (didaktikos) is also used by the Apostle Paul in *2 Timothy 2:24-26*. *"And the Lord's servant must not quarrel; instead, he must be kind to everyone, able to teach, not resentful. 25. Those who oppose him he must gently instruct, in the hope that God will grant them repentance leading them to a knowledge of the truth, 26. and that they will come to their senses and escape from the trap of the devil, who has taken them captive to do his will."*

There the word is grouped with other designations that clearly refer to quality and manner of life. A spiritual leader is to communicate Christ with his entire life. His attitude, industry, integrity, and behavior, all speak of his devotion to Christ. In other words, he teaches by example. He is an epistle of truth and life!

Not addicted to wine (*1 Timothy 3:2,3; Titus 1:7*)
The Spiritual leader must not be given to wine: not be a drunkard, not sit around drinking all the time. In order to justify their right to drink. Some argue that drinking wine was a common practice in the ancient world, even among true Christian believers. However we must always remember what William Barclay so forcefully points out about the ancient world. (a) The water supply was often inadequate and dangerous. (b) Although the ancient world used wine as the commonest of all drinks, they used it with moderation. When wine was drunk, it was drunk in the proportion of two parts of wine to three parts of water. A man who was drunk would be disgraced in ordinary heathen society, let alone in the Church (Note: Proverbs 23:19-21; 29-34)

In a culture like ours where drunkenness is prevalent, the spiritual leader will do well to avoid any conduct that could cause reproach to the work of God. Paul's admonition to the Ephesians puts the matter in positive perspective, *"Do not get drunk on wine, which leads to debauchery. Instead, be filled with the Spirit."–Ephesians 5:18.*

Not self willed *(Titus 1:7)*

An effective spiritual leader is one who works well with others. If he finds an idea that runs counter to his personal desires, but is best for the entire groups, he willingly accepts it. He puts others before himself and avoids "mind sets'. He is a team man that looks at controversial issues with an open, objective mind.

Not quick tempered *(Titus 1:7)*

Paul warns Titus to avoid men who have quick tempers; who are given to sudden bursts of anger. Sinful anger has it's roots in revenge and bitterness. It feeds on resentment. Every spiritual leader must practice self control. He must rule his spirit and learn to hold his tongue from expressions of anger and vindictiveness.

Not pugnacious [Striker]*(Titus 1:7)*

The King James Version has captured the meaning of the Greek word "Plaktan" by translating it "Striker," one who physically lashes out at another. Here Paul speaks not of anger verbalized, but of anger out of control physically. God calls his servant to humility, self control and peace. Vented anger is not to be tolerated.

Not quarrelsome *(1 Timothy 3:2,3)*

The Greek word that is translated here means "Amaichos," which means Peaceable." The man of God is called to peace and not contention.

Gentle *(1 Timothy 3:2,3)*

Paul tells the man of God to be gentle. The original word "Epeikais" means "yielding, gentle, kind, forbearing." All men are called to follow Jesus. He is the model. No man ever demonstrated such gentle spirit as He. In the midst of mocking, slander, ridicule, Jesus responded with gentleness and forbearance.

Free from the love of money *(1 Timothy 3:2,3)*
The word behind this phrase is "Aphilarguron." It is comprised of three parts: a-no; phil-love; arguron-silver, money. The admonition is pointed. Paul tells the spiritual leaders: "Don't love money." Jesus taught, *"Where your treasure is, there will your heart be also." (Matthew 6:21)* The man of God must place his treasures under the control of Christ. All that he possesses must be viewed as a God-given resource, given so it might be given back.

One who manages his household well *(1 Timothy 3:2, 4-5)*
(Vs. 5. "If anyone does not know how to manage his own family, how can he take care of God's church?") *The measure of a man is his family. A man who has proven his leadership in the home will likely prove his leadership in the church. The home is the real test. The standard is high because the responsibility is great. The call is for men who are "strong leaders" at home, for those will be "strong leaders" in the church.*

A good reputation with those outside. *(1 Timothy 3:7)*
The responsibilities of spiritual leaders reach beyond the walls of the church building.
They live under the eye of the community at large. Their testimony of Christ must have a clear ring out there as well. *"Conduct yourself with wisdom...let your speech always be with grace...keep your behavior excellent..., lead quiet life and attend to your own business...behave properly to outsiders..." (Colossians 4:5-6; 1 Peter 2:12; 1 Thessalonians 4:11-12 [NASB])*

Loving what is good. *(Titus 1:7,8)*
Love what is good. The call is for men trained and exercised in this vocation. Men who can look at impossibilities and see the possible, at the hopeless and see hope, at the fallen and see restoration.

Just. *(Titus 1:7,8)*
This is a call for spiritual maturity, for men who have the psychological and spiritual balance to make "just" decisions. Fairness and equity are necessities for effective spiritual leadership, and God's people have a right to demand its presence in their leaders.

Devout. [Holy] *(Titus 1:7,8)*
The original word here is "Hosios" meaning devout, pious, Holy, pleasing to God." The accent here is on God's choosing of a man's life—he is set aside for the work and pleasure of the Lord. This word means to be separated from sin and from all evil, and from immoral, wicked and lawless behavior. Jesus Christ is "Holy" (Hosios): Jesus Christ is perfectly and eternally set apart from sin and free from all immoral and lawless behavior. Jesus Christ is absolutely Holy.

Not a new convert—Not a novice *(1 Timothy 3:6)*
"He must not be a recent convert, or he may become conceited and fall under the same judgment as the devil."

Paul admonishes Timothy to refrain from choosing new converts to fill places of spiritual leadership. The scripture holds forth high standards for spiritual leadership, but that is as it should be, for there is no work on earth so important to time and eternity as the building of Christ's kingdom through His body, the church.

It is very important that the spiritual leader has been a convert for a long time;
* To have become rooted and grounded in the Lord and His Word.
* To become spiritual mature.
* To have proven his testimony for Christ.
* To be known and respected by other believers.
* To be able to minister to others, and teach them to minister.

'...*or he may become conceited and fall under the same judgment as the devil.*"

We need to remember, Satan was expelled from heaven because of pride. When a person is given the great responsibility of becoming a Spiritual leader, before he has become rooted and grounded in the faith, he is most likely going to fall and become condemned just as Satan fell and was condemned.

Filled with the Holy Spirit. (Acts 2:4, 6:3; Ephesians 5:18)
A spiritual leader is…, or is earnestly and actively seeking to be filled with the Holy Spirit.

In total agreement with and supportive…(1 Corinthians 1:10)
"I appeal to you, brothers, in the name of our Lord Jesus Christ, that all of you agree with one another so that there may be no divisions among you and that you may be perfectly united in mind and thought."

"Every kingdom divided against it self will be ruined, and every city or household divided against itself will not stand.–Matthew 12:25

Spiritual leaders who are serving at the same fellowship ought to promote unity, and be in total agreement with, and supportive of the tenets of faith, and statements of fundamental truths of the fellowship where you are a part of, as long as they are in agreement with the written Word of God. And promote obedience to the Will of God.

Being a member of the Body of Christ

The body is a unit, though it is made up of many parts; and though all its parts are many, they form one body. So it is with Christ. For we were all baptized by one Spirit into one body whether Jews or Greeks, slave or free, and we were all given the one Spirit to drink. Now the body is not made up of one part but of many. 1 Corinthians 12:12-14

As a Christian, you have certain responsibilities toward God and toward other believers. When you received Jesus Christ as Savior and Lord, you became a member of the universal, or "invisible," church. You belong to "the family of believers" (Galatians 6:10) and are part of the body of Christ. Since we belong to Jesus Christ and his universal church, we have the responsibility of obeying him and joining a local manifestation of that body.

Through ministering in churches of different denominations I learned that there are many different views on this, but I do believe that is important to mention, that the choice of making an commitment to the fellowship of your choosing does not only bless you, but also brings a great responsibility

The writer to the Hebrews stated, *"Let us not give up meeting together, as some are in the habit of doing, but let us encourage one another, and all the more as you see the day approaching"* (Hebrews 10:25).

Some personal thoughts about selecting a Christian fellowship:

The church of your choosing ought to be a Bible believing and Christ Centered fellowship

Jesus answered, "I am the way and the truth and the life. No one comes to the Father except through me.–John 14:6

"'...then know this, you and all the people of Israel: It is by the name of Jesus Christ of Nazareth, whom you crucified but whom God raised from the dead, that this man stands before you healed. He is "'the stone you builders rejected, which has become the capstone.' Salvation is found in no one else, for there is no other name under heaven given to men by which we must be saved."– Acts 4:10-12

To make sure we do not end up in a cult, following men's opinions, dreams and visions which are contrary to God's truth, it would be wise to examine where the church stand in their believes.

When talking about being Christ Centered, we do not just talk about Him, but we acknowledge Him in our midst. We have an attitude of submission to one another out of reverence for Christ. (Ephesians 5:21)

For where two or three come together in my name, there am I with them."–Matthew 18:20

A truly Christ Centered church Invites His presence in the form of the Holy Spirit, and let Him give them new revelations of Himself through His Word. No vision, prophesy or interpretation is more valid then that what is written in the Word of God—the Bible!

Do not put out the Spirit's fire; do not treat prophecies with contempt. Test everything. Hold on to the good. Avoid every kind of evil. May God himself, the God of peace, sanctify you through and through. May your whole spirit, soul and body be kept blameless at the coming of our Lord Jesus Christ. The one who calls you is faithful and he will do it.–1 Thessalonians 5:19-24

This church allows the Holy Spirit to empower the body of Christ in their Christian walk, by distributing the body the gifts of the Holy Spirit. The leadership of this church gives the body the freedom to operate in their gifts without having them drawing attention to them selves. It is important that there remains always order in the church, with the evidence of godly fruit being released.

But the fruit of the Spirit is love, joy, peace, patience, kindness, goodness, faithfulness, gentleness and self-control. Against such things there is no law. Those who belong to Christ Jesus have crucified the sinful nature with its passions and desires. Since we live by the Spirit, let us keep in step with the Spirit. Let us not become conceited, provoking and envying each other.–Galatians 5:22-26

The church should promote Holiness, and right living. It should have the fundamentals of faith you can agree with, stand behind, and have peace about.

Therefore, since Christ suffered in his body, arm yourselves also with the same attitude, because he who has suffered in his body is done with sin. As a result, he does not live the rest of his earthly life for evil human desires, but rather for the will of God.–1 Peter 4: 1-2

Because of the many different Christian points of view of translating the scriptures, and their different forms of worship, I encourage anyone to go, where they feel led by the Holy Spirit.

Watch your life and doctrine closely. Persevere in them, because if you do, you will save both yourself and your hearers.–1Timothy 4:16

We need to keep in mind that when we join a church to belong, we go to strengthen the body, and not to change it to our own likings.
Speak to one another with psalms, hymns and spiritual songs. Sing and make music in your heart to the Lord, always giving thanks to God the Father for everything, in the name of our Lord Jesus Christ. Submit to one another out of reverence for Christ.–Ephesians 5:19-21

Going to a church, with the desire to change it to your ideas, could create division, and that are one of the things that God hates.

There are six things the LORD hates, seven that are detestable to him: haughty eyes, a lying tongue, hands that shed innocent blood, a heart that devises wicked schemes, feet that are quick to rush into evil, a false witness who pours out lies and a man who stirs up dissension among brothers.–Proverbs 6:17-19

The church must provide an opportunity for its members to glorify God and to worship him.

Because of the many forms of worship, it could be easy to become attached to our own style. We need to remember that we are not to worship, "worship" or the instruments of worship, but God Himself. Genuine worship is a giving to God, what we know He would like to receive from us.

He who sacrifices thank offerings honors me, and he prepares the way so that I may show him the salvation of God."–Psalm 50:23

God is Spirit and his worshipers must worship in spirit and in truth."– John 4:24

Therefore, I urge you, brothers, in view of God's mercy, to offer your bodies as living sacrifices, holy and pleasing to God—this is your spiritual act of worship.–Romans 12:1

The church should provide the greatest opportunity for personal and family growth.

The congregation of your choosing must provide a place for strengthening our faith, and gives you confidence in your Christian walk. It is a place where we can be in unity, receiving support and encouragement from each other to become all that God wants us to be.

Have nothing to do with godless myths and old wives' tales; rather, train yourself to be godly. For physical training is of some value, but godliness has value for all things, holding promise for both the present life and the life to come.–1Timothy 4:7-8

And without faith it is impossible to please God, because anyone who comes to him must believe that he exists and that he rewards those who earnestly seek him.–Hebrews 11:6

The church should have a vision you feel can stand behind and can be a part of.

Joining a Christian fellowship is not only filling a chair, or a pew on the day we visit the church. It is about joining their mission, to reach out to each other, and together reach out to the world.

Where there is no vision, the people cast off restraint; But he that keeps the law, happy is he.–Proverbs 29:18

The church should offer an opportunity to be involved in carrying out the Great Commission.

Jesus said: "The harvest is plentiful, but the workers are few. Ask the Lord of the harvest, therefore, to send out workers into his harvest field. Go! I am sending you out like lambs among wolves."–Luke 10:2-3

Being a part of the great commission begins on our knees. One of the most important tools in fulfilling this call is to pray. To pray for souls to get saved, for their needs to be met, and for workers to be send.

The reality is that not everybody is capable to be involved in fulltime ministry. But we can sure do our part. We can stand behind those who can go, by praying for them, and when possible by financially supporting them.

However, when we are able to be physically involved in ministry, lets not just look at the need and pray, but let us also roll up our sleeves and be a part of the solution.

Then Jesus came to them and said, "All authority in heaven and on earth has been given to me. Therefore go and make disciples of all nations, baptizing them in the name of the Father and of the Son and of the Holy Spirit, and teaching them to obey everything I have commanded you. And surely I am with you always, to the very end of the age."– Matthew 28: 18-20

The church should provide opportunities for Christian service.

Jesus Christ, who gave himself for us to redeem us from all wickedness and to purify for himself a people that are his very own, eager to do what is good.–Titus 2:13-14

The end of all things is near. Therefore be clear minded and self-controlled so that you can pray. Above all, love each other deeply, because love covers over a multitude of sins. Offer hospitality to one another without grumbling. Each one should use whatever gift he has received to serve others, faithfully administering God's grace in its various forms. If anyone speaks, he should do it as one speaking the very words of God. If anyone serves, he should do it with the strength God provides, so that in all things God may be praised through Jesus Christ. To him be the glory and the power for ever and ever. Amen. 1 Peter 4:7-11

The church must provide a place and opportunity for fellowship for its members.

As Christian disciples we should look forward to the next contact we have with believing friends and members of our church. We have seen how the social life of the early Church was centered around the gathering together of the believers.

I believe a healthy church ought to be kind of like a green house, offering the right light, the right food, and the right temperature where people can grow, become healthy, and become strong and fruitful.

Make every effort to live in peace with all men and to be holy; without holiness no one will see the Lord.–Hebrews 12:14

Next to our regular church services, we should also look for time and opportunity to have fun together. We should invite each other in our homes for a meal, or refreshments. Perhaps you could go fishing or hunting together, play a round of golf, or go bowling with a couple of families.

This kind of events would also open up opportunities to invite the non-Christian.

Through this kind of fellowship new relationships could be established, and times for sharing your Christian testimonies will be made possible. This could also a great opportunity to include the un-saved spouse, or the children of the person who is saved already. Good relationships are valued by everybody, and are hard to come by.

Two are better than one, because they have a good return for their work: If one falls down, his friend can help him up. But pity the man who falls and has no one to help him up! Also, if two lie down together, they will keep warm. But how can one keep warm alone? Though one may be overpowered, two can defend themselves. A cord of three strands is not quickly broken.–Ecclesiastes 4:9-12

"...Encourage one another daily, as long as it is called today, so that none of you may be hardened by sin's deceitfulness.–Hebrews 3:13

The church must provide an opportunity to give financially, physically, and practically.

The Scriptures teach us that we are to give our tithe for the furtherance of the ministry of God's church, and help those who are in need. Next to our giving from our finances, we should consider giving some of our time to serve in or outside the church.

Jesus said, "If anyone has ears to hear, let him hear. Consider carefully what you hear," he continued. "With the measure you use, it will be measured to you—and even more. Whoever has will be given more; whoever does not have, even what he has will be taken from him."–Mark 4:23-25

When Jesus founded the church, he intended his followers to join it and remain faithful to it. If you have committed yourself to being one of Christ's 21st-century disciples, then associate yourself with a local congregation. But be sure it is a church that is committed to carrying out the Great Commission. The reality is, you need the church and the church needs you. When you are willing to commit to a body of committed believers, they then will be able to commit to you too.

Summery: A healthy Christian fellowship encourages Spiritual growth.

Whenever a group of Christians meets together for Bible study, a time of prayer, or a discussion of the Scriptures, there must be a challenge to growth that each person can respond to.

Fellowship Must Involve Sharing Jesus Christ with One Another. Sharing of Christ between Christians includes victories and joys of submission and obedience to the word of God. It means sharing the joy of knowing that we are walking in the center of his will. It is sharing what we are getting out of our quiet time each morning. It is telling other believers of the blessings we have received, the provision God has made for our needs, and his marvelous answers to our prayers.

A healthy Christian fellowship encourages practical evangelistic ministry.

Jesus said: *"He who is not with Me is against Me, and he who does not gather with Me scatters abroad"–Matthew 12:30.*

Perhaps you have experienced the excitement of seeing people come to Christ and then become involved in a challenging fellowship with other believers. As a result of that exposure, they have been getting into God's word and in a short while become concerned for their friends who are still lost. They want them to come to know the Savior as they have done. Some great events to promote fellowship outside of the church building could be fishing, hunting, bowling, playing golf, or to have lunch together.

A healthy Christian fellowship encourages Discipleship ministry.

As iron sharpens iron, so one man sharpens another.–Proverbs 27:17

Genuine fellowship results in bringing each other the needed encouragement, the necessary correction, and becoming the kind of person God wants us to become.

All of us get tired and discouraged, and need physical and Biblical encouragement from others. King David had a word of encouragement for his son Solomon. *"Be strong and courageous, and do the work. Do not be afraid or discouraged, for the Lord God, my God, is with you. He will not fail you or forsake you until all the work for the service of the temple of the Lord is finished"–1 Chronicles 28:20.*

Whenever our parents, leaders, or those over us speak like that, we are greatly encouraged. For all of us need encouragement, and the place to receive it is in the fellowship to which we belong. When a person is without fellowship, he may not realize he is deviating from the straight and narrow. The writer to the Hebrews wrote:

"See to it, brothers, that none of you has a sinful, unbelieving heart that turns away from the living God. But encourage one another daily, as long as it is called Today, so that none of you may be hardened by sin's deceitfulness" (Hebrews 3:12-13).

Sin always shows its effects in our life. When these effects are visible to others in our fellowship by those who know the Lord, they then are able to help us to change them. They can minister to us a word of correction or rebuke and help us recognize how important it is to deal with such things. We then need the humility to recognize our need for change and to submit to their teachings.

A healthy Christian fellowship encourages people to be personally involved in foreign missions.

Therefore go and make disciples of all nations, baptizing them in the name of the Father and of the Son and of the Holy Spirit, and teaching them to obey everything I have commanded you. And surely I am with you always, to the very end of the age."–Matthew 28:19-20

God is calling us to have a world vision. We ought to spread the Good News however and where ever we can. And after we have done that, we need to teach and encourage those who have accepted the Gospel to do the same. We need to support the missionary, but also let those they minister too know that we are standing with them, that we are praying for them, and that we love them.

A few years ago, my wife and I went to India; there we learned that the people we met had not received any Biblical encouragement for about four years. They were unable to read or write, and still were repeating the same stories they had ones heard them selves. Many of these Christians felt forsaken and had prayed for God to send them someone who would teach them more about God.

Today, because of the internet, mobile solar or crank operated cassette players and support from missionaries, they are able to learn, and to have fellowship on a regular basis.

All of us need other Christians in our lives, to encourage, and sometimes correct us in our Christian walk if we are to survive in this hostile world.

A healthy Christian fellowship encourages each person to become all that they ought to be.

Solomon wrote long ago, "He who walks with the wise grows wise, but a companion of fools suffers harm" (Proverbs 13:20).

If you are in mutual communion and fellowship with others who know the Savior and who are committed to his lordship, then you will grow and increase in the depth of your relationship with Jesus Christ and with one another. Fellowship is as important to our spiritual life as exercise is to our physical body. Multitudes of Christians have been nurtured and cared for within a body of believers. It is important for the local church and its leadership to be committed to helping the people under their care grow in the Lord and experience the fellowship that the Bible calls all believers to.

I want to encourage you, make fellowship an integral part of your life. Make sure it is Christ-centered and motivates you to reach out to those around you who do not know the Savior. It must be one that encourages you, provides correction when you need it, and helps you become the person Christ intended and enables you to be.

I believe that all Christians, young and old, must be plugged into a local church so that the body of believers can be a source of nourishment for their spiritual growth.

We need to fellowship with other believers, displaying love and unity.

Christian fellowship is an absolute necessity in the life of every believer, whether it is totally tied to a local church or includes other interchurch activities. For many Christians the only fellowship they experience is provided by their local congregation.

Fellowship is carried on wherever a body of believers gathers together. Whenever a Christian is isolated from others who have a similar relationship with Jesus Christ, there is something missing from his or her life. Even though that person may have fellowship with Christ through the word and prayer, the mutual encouragement and strengthening that comes from association with other believers in the Lord is missing.

It is important that we understand the meaning of the word "fellowship" because it is the key to understanding what the biblical concept of Christian fellowship is.

The Greek term *koinonia* is used throughout the Scriptures and is translated into English consistently as "fellowship." *Koinonia* means "sharing in something with someone."

A careful study of the New Testament use of this word-group indicates that Christian koinonia or "commonness" takes three forms.

It speaks of our common inheritance–what we share in together

Of our co-operative service—what we share out together,
Of our reciprocal responsibility-what we share with one another.

Each one of us as a Christian has much to share with other fellow believers. If we were to make a list, it would be endless. We should share our daily experiences with Jesus Christ' guidance and forgiveness, the ministry of helping others grow in Christ, our efforts in evangelism, and insights on teaching Sunday school classes.

One of the blessings of our fellowship together is that as we share our walk with Jesus Christ, we can encourage other believers who may be going through some problems we have experienced.

In fact, the Apostle Paul taught that God *"comforts us in all our troubles, so that we can comfort those in any trouble with the comfort we ourselves have received from God"–2 Corinthians 1:4.*

A beautiful illustration of fellowship may be seen in the experience of the early Church. The passage found in Acts 2:42-47, gives an excellent example of true fellowship, this together with a clear description of the training or instruction which the new converts received within the local body of believers.

God was certainly honored in the early Church as the believers displayed love and unity. Glory comes to God from this kind of fellowship, for out of it is born a living, powerful witness that causes men and women to fall to their knees and acknowledge Jesus Christ as Savior and Lord of their life.

The Apostle John stated that the source of fellowship was a relationship with the Lord. *"We proclaim to you what we have seen and heard, so that you also may have fellowship with us. And our fellowship is with the Father and with his Son, Jesus Christ"–1 John 1:3.*

John knew what it was to have an intimate relationship with the Lord. He had heard him, seen him, and even touched him (see 1 John 1:1). During Jesus' ministry, John had a close relationship with Jesus; he had talked with him and had shared his heart with him.

John then invited his readers to join with him in that fellowship with Jesus. The basis of Christian fellowship is the relationship that we individually have with God through Jesus Christ. It is only because of that relationship that we can have fellowship with one another within the body of Christ. And because the other person also has a dynamic relationship with the Lord, we profit from it and experience the encouragement and mutual sharing that is so necessary for all of us.

It is impossible for Christians to have true biblical fellowship with people who do not know Jesus Christ. Even though they may be our relatives and friends, dearly loved and respected by us, we cannot experience the biblical fellowship that we need unless they know Jesus Christ personally.

Love and unity also are absolute necessities if there is going to be true biblical fellowship.

We love because he first loved us. If anyone says, "I love God," yet hates his brother, he is a liar. For anyone who does not love his brother, whom he has seen, cannot love God, whom he has not seen. And he has given us this command: Whoever loves God must also love his brother.– 1 John 4:19-21

Paul wrote to one of his churches, *"If you have any encouragement from being united with Christ, if any comfort from his love, if any fellowship with the Spirit, if any tenderness and compassion, then make my joy complete by being like-minded, having the same love, being one in spirit and purpose"–Philippians 2:1-2.*

For true fellowship to take place there must be love and unity among the participants. There is no disunity or lack of love when the Holy Spirit is in control.

When a group of Christians have surrendered to the will of God and are letting the Holy Spirit control their lives and govern their situations, the result will be Christian fellowship. In our relationships with other Christians we have to love one another and maintain the unity of the Holy Spirit.

The foundation of discipleship

"Love never fails. But where there are prophecies, they will cease; where there are tongues, they will be stilled; where there is knowledge, it will pass away..."–1 Corinthians 13:8

In his last ministry to the disciples before the cross, Jesus told them, *"A new commandment I give you: Love one another. As I have loved you, so you must love one another. All men will know that you are my disciples if you love one another"–John 13:34-35.*

This love of which Jesus was speaking includes putting the interests and concerns of other people ahead of ours. One of the practical ways in which this may be done is to call a friend, especially one who might be undergoing some testing or difficulties. Visit with him for a while, then share a verse of Scripture as a word of encouragement and assure him that you are praying for him. Share some of the victories that God is giving you personally. These few moments spent on the phone with a Christian brother will involve you in real fellowship.

Following the lifestyle of Jesus we learn that:

Jesus manifested His love through His attitude of perfect-self forgetfulness.

"For God so loved the world that he gave his one and only Son, that whoever believes in him shall not perish but have eternal life.–John 3:16;

Jesus gave is life for us, knowing that we did not deserve it, or even appreciate at times.

His message to us:

Be imitators of God, therefore, as dearly loved children and live a life of love, just as Christ loved us and gave himself up for us as a fragrant offering and sacrifice to God–Ephesians 5:1-2

Jesus manifested His love through His attitude of humility and servant hood.

"Come to me, all you who are weary and burdened, and I will give you rest. Take my yoke upon you and learn from me, for I am gentle and humble in heart, and you will find rest for your souls. For my yoke is easy and my burden is light."–Matthew 11:28-30

When he had finished washing their feet, he put on his clothes and returned to his place. "Do you understand what I have done for you?" he asked them. "You call me 'Teacher' and 'Lord,' and rightly so, for that is what I am. Now that I, your Lord and Teacher, have washed your feet, you also should wash one another's feet. I have set you an example that you should do as I have done for you. I tell you the truth, no servant is greater than his master, nor is a messenger greater than the one who sent him. Now that you know these things, you will be blessed if you do them.– John 13:12-17

Jesus, even though he was the son of God, The King of Kings, He was willing to be the least, and assumed the attitude of a servant.

Jesus manifested His love through His Persistent effort to raise the worst

For God did not send his Son into the world to condemn the world, but to save the world through him.–John 3:17;

Jesus, knowing all things, could easy become a expert in finding fault, and criticize those around Him, but nevertheless he choose to see the best and the potential in them.

Jesus manifested His love through His attitude of forgiveness toward those who mistreated Him

Jesus said, *"Father, forgive them, for they do not know what they are doing."–Luke 23:34*

Being falsely accused, horribly physical abused, forsaken by his friends, ridiculed, and hanging on the cross to die, Jesus still had it in Him to forgive those who were gambling a way is clothes.

Jesus, while teaching us to pray, said:

"This, then, is how you should pray: "'Our Father in heaven, hallowed be your name, your kingdom come, your will be done on earth as it is in heaven. Give us today our daily bread. Forgive us our debts, as we also have forgiven our debtors. And lead us not into temptation, but deliver us from the evil one. 'For if you forgive men when they sin against you, your heavenly Father will also forgive you.–Matthew 6:9-14

12 Ways to Hurt Your Church

1. Don't attend. **2.** If you do attend, arrive late and leave early. **3.** Visit other churches often. **4.** At every service ask your self, "What's in it for me "? **5.** Never volunteer for anything. Let the pastor or others do it. **6.** Gossip. **7.** Be critical of the pastor and the musicians. **8.** Don't tithe or give any love offerings, or wait until the end of the tax year to see if you have any extra money. **9.** Don't talk with others or encourage them. **10.** Don't forgive when someone offends you. **11.** Avoid praying for your church. **12.** Behave as a saint in the church, but as a pagan in daily life.

8. Following After Jesus

To this you were called, because Christ suffered for you, leaving you an example that you should follow in His footsteps.–I Peter 2:21

Following my salvation experience I did a lot of growing in the Lord. I become a member of a full-gospel church, received a Bible education and got very active in practical evangelism and discipleship.

It was several years of this process before I met my wife JoAnne.

She was an American missionary working with Youth With A Mission (YWAM) in Amsterdam the Netherlands. She had been raised in a Mennonite home, and after God had filled her with the Holy Spirit, He had called her to be a missionary to my country. Later somehow throughout a mixture of circumstances our ministries crossed paths together, and we got married with the desire to minister in unison as the Lord would lead

It was in the fall of 1983, that God spoke to our heart to go to the United States to missionaries. With the desire to follow up on this we found ourselves facing several obstacles.

One was I needed a visa. Another; I needed a plane ticked what cost money we did not have. I had a newly furnished rental apartment, and had accrued a debt of several thousand dollars in doing so. But we trusted God enough that when he wanted us to go, He would meet the needs. As we started to pray about those needs, we saw God move very quickly—at least that is what we thought at that time.

When sharing our needs about our adventure with our friends and pastor it seemed that they were all very excited for us, and believed with us that this was the right thing to do.

Only a Week after sharing with them it appeared that all the pieces would be coming together. Two of our best friends had quickly approached us and said that they believed they ought to come and live in our apartment while we would be in the US, and that when our year of missions was up we could have it back. At the same time they would take care of the debt we had. Besides, they were the ones who could enjoy the benefit of using our new purchased furniture, carpet and kitchen utensils.

We were very excited, and in good faith we continued in getting ready for the trip.

However, with about one week before our planned departure when our preparations should have been in order, it seemed to fall apart before us. At our apartment on Saturday evening about seven o'clock, we received some visitors. Our two best friends, the ones who had told us that they were going to take care of our apartment and our debt came to see us.

Seeing them a little nervous and fidgety we asked what was going on. They then told us that what ever they had previously promised us was not going to happen. They had lost their peace about it.

I can tell you it was as if somebody pulled the rug from under us. I do not remember much more about the conversation that followed, or when they left. I do know that we were shocked. The next day going to church we were the last ones to come in, and the first ones to leave. We did not want to talk to anyone about the things that had happened. That Sunday afternoon, my wife and I went for a quiet walk on the beach. Normally when we went to the beach, walking the dog, we would sing and pray together at leisure, but this time we were just walking, still trying to collect our thoughts. It was when we were about at the end of our walk that we said to each other, "Let's pray and ask God what He wants us to do next." While telling God about our feelings of disappointment and hurt, telling Him that we choose to forgive our friends for letting us down this because we did not want any of our bad feelings interfere what God mite wanted to do next, we went home.

It was about seven o'clock that Sunday evening; we just had finished eating, that the door bell rang again. Not knowing what to expect next we opened the door, and saw that we were visited by an older woman together with a young man, who were later introduced to us as mother and her son. These were people we had never met before, and until this very day I still do not know how they learned about us, or how they knew where we lived. And in the things that followed, I am not even sure we asked. We were far too overwhelmed by what was taken place.

When we asked how we could help them, the mother asked us, "Are you the people who are going to the United States?" After we confirmed this plan, she continued, "I am here to buy up all your furniture, and I want to take over the apartment for my son, and when you agree, you can stay living here until the end of next week."—This was the exact time we were planning to fly to our new mission field.

Even though we did not have the required visa to enter the USA, or the money to purchase the plane ticked I needed, and despite the fact that we did not now where we would live when the vision to go to the USA failed, we agreed, and she paid us cash all the money we needed to pay of the debt.

Looking back at this, it seemed that the first step of faith, seeing all our needs met, and to be able to follow up on the assignment God had given us, was to let go of everything we were trying to hold on to. The Thursday following, after my physical I received my visa, and the next day several hours before the closing time of the travel agency God blessed us with the money I needed to get my plane ticked. When the day of departure came, we knew that He who called us to follow Him is faithful!

In the book of John, Jesus spoke to the people, and said, *"I am the light of the world. Whoever follows me will never walk in darkness, but will have the light of life."–John 8:12.*

Jesus talks of following Him, and we often speak of following Jesus, because of this statement by Jesus. But what does it really mean?

The Greek word for "follows" is "akoloutheo." This word has 5 different, but closely connected meanings.

It is often used of a soldier following his captain's orders and given direction.
The soldier follows wherever the captain may lead, on long marches, into battle, or on maneuvers in foreign countries. A Christian disciple is the soldier whose commander is Jesus Christ.

This word is often used about a slave who is following (traveling with) his master. Wherever the master goes, the slave is there to serve him or to carry out the task which the master gave him to do. The slave is literally always at his master's disposal.

The Christian disciple is the slave whose joy it is always to serve Jesus Christ.

The word "akoloutheo" is used when someone is following up or accepting a wise counselor's opinion. When a man needs counsel, he will seek direction from an expert in that area, and if he is wise, he will accept the guidance he receives. The Christian disciple is the one who directs his life and follows the counsel of Jesus Christ.

This word is used to describe obedience to the law of a country or city. To be a useful member of society, he must agree to follow the laws of the land. Christian disciples are citizens of the kingdom of Heaven and need to accept the law of Jesus Christ and the kingdom of God.

This word is used to describe a student who is following his teacher's explanation of the lesson or following someone who is presenting a story.

The Christian disciple is one who follows and understands the lessons and teachings of Jesus.

To follow Jesus is to surrender your body, soul & spirit in obedience to Jesus, doing that, what we know Jesus was doing.

Jesus said: "I tell you the truth, anyone who has faith in me will do what I have been doing. He will do even greater things than these, because I am going to the Father."–John 14: 12,

The big question

"What was He doing that He expects us to follow-up on?

"I believe that one example could be found in the book of Luke, where Jesus is saying:

"The Spirit of the Lord is on me, because he has anointed me to preach good news to the poor. He has sent me to proclaim freedom for the prisoners and recovery of sight for the blind, to release the oppressed, to proclaim the year of the Lord's favor."
–Luke 4:18-20

Jesus was filled, and surrendered to the leading of the Holy Spirit.
He had chosen to follow the path what was laid before Him in the power of the Holy Spirit. He laid down His live to save others. He prayed before His capture and crucifixion:

"Father, if you are willing, take this cup from me; yet not my will, but yours be done." –Luke 22:42

Jesus was anointed to: Preach the Good news to the Poor
Jesus did not look at the financial status of the people, but to their inward need. Those who experienced a spiritual poverty.

Jesus was anointed to: Heal the broken hearted
He was ministering to those who feel as if nobody understands or cares. Those who feel lonely and abandoned ; forsaken. Those who are crushed by grief; blemished or violated by sin. Overcome by rejection, Guild, and hate of self…

Jesus was anointed to: Bring deliverance to the captives
The Bible say's, *"In him we have redemption through his blood, the forgiveness of sins, in accordance with the riches of God's grace"*– Ephesians 1:7

The Bible teaches us that before we give our lives to God, we are held captive by sin.
If your find yourself a slave to some vice, or sin, something you simply can't overcome,
Jesus wants to set you free!

He told us in *"I tell you the truth, whatever you bind on earth will be bound in heaven, and whatever you loose on earth will be loosed in heaven. "Again, I tell you that if two of you on earth agree about anything you ask for, it will be done for you by my Father in heaven. For where two or three come together in my name, there am I with them."–Matt. 18:18-20;*

Jesus was anointed to give sight to the blind

He is not just talking about those who are physical blind. In many cases, the Devil has blinded the minds of those who are Saved and NOT saved. His purpose is to limit Biblical understanding.

The sad story is that according to the statistics recorded in the Pentecostal Evangel of December 24 /2006, that among the National population in the USA, only 35% believe that the scriptures are the actual Word of God. Among the Pentecostal's it is about 76%; The Charismatic's 48%–; and among other Christians there are only 37% of them who believe that the scriptures are actual Word of God

This means that among all those Christians only a small percentage recognize God's Word as their ultimate form of authority.

The main reason of this could be that many of these people have no genuine understanding of the Word and Way's of God.

These sobering statistics reminds us, that we, who know the truth, need to take the responsibility of teaching the truth to the people around us very seriously.

"...dear friends, build yourselves up in your most holy faith and pray in the Holy Spirit. Keep yourselves in God's love as you wait for the mercy of our Lord Jesus Christ to bring you to eternal life. Be merciful to those who doubt; snatch others from the fire and save them; to others show mercy, mixed with fear—hating even the clothing stained by corrupted flesh. –Jude 20-23

Jesus was anointed to: Bring liberty to the oppressed and the Down trodden

Those who are crushed with life–Overcome with worries and burdens.

Jesus was anointed to: to proclaim the year of the Lord's favor."
For he says, "In the time of my favor I heard you, and in the day of salvation I helped you." I tell you, now is the time of God's favor, now is the day of salvation.–2 Corinthians 6:2

Jesus was anointed to preach the era of salvation–Not Judgment, for that will be His future ministry where we will judge the world.–But he was anointed to bring salvation of all men.

"For God so loved the world that he gave his one and only Son, that whoever believes in him shall not perish but have eternal life. For God did not send his Son into the world to condemn the world, but to save the world through him.–John 3:16-17

9. A Personal Relationship with Christ

In Revelations 3:20, Jesus say's: *"Here I am! I stand at the door and knock. If anyone hears my voice and opens the door, I will come in and eat with him, and he with me."*

Having had my first known encounter with God, would make you think that, from that time it is easy to repeat them. Well I have learned throughout the years that it requires a lot of commitment, effort and persistence. God is not a person who pushes Himself on you; we have to pursue Him. Gods said:

"You will seek me and find me when you seek me with all your heart."– Jeremiah 29:13

I have to admit, to have a relationship with Jesus can be frustrating sometimes, especially when you are in a hurry, but He seems to take it slow. When you wish that God would speak so loud that you can not miss it, it seems that God speaks a gentle whisper (1 Kings 19:12). And oh yes, there are times that you are bombarded with so many thoughts, impressions, opinions, and voices, that it is hard to even identify what God mite be trying to say to you.

Throughout the years I learned that to hear the gentle whispering voice of Jesus:

We need to start by tuning in.

Many times we are missing the voice of God because we are not ready to listen. We need to make the choice to concentrate / discipline / focus our selves, to tune in our hearts / mind and our ears, and listen for the voice of God. [Turn on your ears like a radio or TV]

We must avoid selective hearing.

"My dear brothers, take note of this: Everyone should be quick to listen, slow to speak and slow to become angry, for man's anger does not bring about the righteous life that God desires. Therefore, get rid of all moral filth and the evil that is so prevalent, and humbly accept the word planted in you, which can save you."–James 1:19-20

We must be willing to be obedient.

Do not merely listen to the word, and so deceive yourselves. Do what it says. Anyone who listens to the word but does not do what it says is like a man who looks at his face in a mirror and, after looking at himself, goes away and immediately forgets what he looks like. But the man who looks intently into the perfect law that gives freedom, and continues to do this, not forgetting what he has heard, but doing it—he will be blessed in what he does.–James 1:21-25

We must develop Spiritual hearing

Did you ever wonder why people doctors recommend you not to play your music to loud in your headset, or… Why many people wear ear protectors on their ears when they are working with power tools? The reason for this is, that the high levels of sound generated by these saws and drills can reduce the sensitivity of our hearing. It can make us hard of hearing!!!

I believe that often, one of the reasons, we have a hard time recognizing, and hearing and understanding the voice of God, because of the sensitivity of our spiritual ears have been damaged by the world's noise. (Radio–TV–etc…) And the only way for us to overcome this, is by pursuing quiet time with God. By taking our Bibles, with us in a quiet place where we can spend quality time in prayer and reading the Word. Expecting to hear His voice, assuming an attitude like Samuel saying, "Speak, for your servant is listening." (1 Samuel 3:10)

Even though there are many other examples found throughout the Bible,

Jesus is making it very clear to us that He desires a personal relationship with His Disciples. It is though this relationship that we will know Him and Understand Him, love Him more, but also grow in our faith. It is His desire that as we received Christ by faith, so we should live by faith daily. And that comes only as we are in the word of God. *"Consequently, faith comes from hearing the message, and the message is heard through the word of Christ"*– Romans 10:17.

We discover as we spend time with God alone, reading and meditating on his word and praying, that he ministers to us through his Holy Spirit and that our faith will grow on a daily basis. Anyone who has a living relationship with God will testify that it is due to the quality of the time he spends in God's word and prayer.

Jesus said: *"My sheep listen to my voice; I know them, and they follow me."*–John 10:27

Jesus had a relationship with the Heavenly Father

The practice of Jesus should be sufficient to show us the importance of our daily devotions. Early in his ministry we find him setting time aside to meet with the Father.

Let's look at the life of Jesus. He seemed pretty busy. While most of us after a day like that would want to stay in bed the next morning. Throughout the ministry of Jesus, most days were filled with activity, but he took the time to rise early in the morning to pray. He had been busy until well after sunset, but he was up before sunrise

Mark records for us, *"Very early in the morning, while it was still dark, Jesus got up, left the house and went off to a solitary place, where he prayed"*–Mark 1:35. The significance of this is obvious when you consider the circumstances of the previous day. Jesus spent time in the synagogue in Capernaum teaching. While there he healed a man who was possessed by an evil spirit. After he left the synagogue, Jesus went to the home of Simon and Andrew. There he healed Simon's mother-in-law. After sunset many people gathered at the home to be healed of various diseases.

The book of Psalms gives us some examples

The Psalms are full of expressions of devotion to the Lord. This means that the men who wrote these marvelous psalms had a vital relationship with him. David wrote: *"Let the morning bring me word of your unfailing love, for I have put my trust in you. Show me the way I should go, for to you I lift up my soul"–Psalm 143:8.*

He also wrote: *"Blessed is the man you choose and bring near to live in your courts! We are filled with the good things of your house, of your holy temple"–Psalm 65:4.*

David pours out his heart about his need for fellowship with God in this psalm: *"O God, you are my God, earnestly I seek you; my soul thirsts for you, my body longs for you, in a dry and weary land where there is no water. I have seen you in the sanctuary and beheld your power and your glory. Because your love is better than life, my lips will glorify you. I will praise you as long as I live, and in your name I will lift up my hands. My soul will be satisfied as with the richest of foods; with singing lips my mouth will praise you. On my bed I remember you; I think of you through the watches of the night. Because you are my help, I sing in the shadow of your wings. I stay close to you; your right hand upholds me."–Psalm 63:1-8.*

Another psalmist wrote, *"It is good to praise the Lord and make music to your name, O Most High, to proclaim your love in the morning and your faithfulness at night"–Psalm 92:1-2.* As you study this passage and others like it, the following pattern emerges; thanking God for his love in the morning and his faithfulness at night.

Jesus Christ Made Fellowship Possible

In Old Testament times in Israel, God ordained that sacrifices be offered morning and evening, a symbolic preview of what Jesus would accomplish on the cross. It was at the mercy seat that God met with his people Israel. But now, every one of us can meet with God on a daily basis. The death of Jesus Christ on the cross of Calvary has provided the basis for our daily fellowship with the living God. Only because of this, it is possible to have communion and fellowship with the holy and righteous God. The writer to the Hebrews declared that we have direct access to God through the merit of Jesus Christ's death on Calvary.

Therefore, brothers, since we have confidence to enter the Most Holy Place by the blood of Jesus, by a new and living way opened for us through the curtain, that is, his body, and since we have a great priest over the house of God, let us draw near to God with a sincere heart in full assurance of faith, having our hearts sprinkled to cleanse us from a guilty conscience and having our bodies washed with pure water– Hebrews 10:19-22.

A while back, during one of my devotions, the Lord spoke to my heart, and said: "Many people come to me but don't enter in. My people are holding back, and because of this, they are missing out on the blessings I have for them. Not understanding what the Lord was trying to teach me, I asked him to explain. He then drew my attention to the Old Testament story of Moses and the picture of the Tabernacle (Exodus 25-30). Here we learn that it was only the High priest, who after a lot of spiritual and physical preparations was to go through the curtain from the Holy place to the Holies of Holy—The place where the mercy seat was located, and in the presence of God.

Here in the book of Hebrews however we learn that, because of what Jesus did for us on the cross, we too may enter through the curtain, in to the presence of God. The thing what the Lord explained to me, is that even though we have the invitation to go through the curtain to be with Him, many of us are still speaking to Him from the opposite site of the curtain.

Some of the reasons of this could be:

We are not sure He is listening; we are in a hurry; we are afraid that He mite asks us to do something, or give up on something we are not ready to surrender. We do not believe that God will answer our prayers; Instead of seeking after God *[Jeremiah 29:11-14]*, we want Him to seek after us; we do not know how to enter in.

God Desires Fellowship with Us

The amazing thing we find in Scripture is that God wants to have fellowship with us.

What a tremendous thought it is to realize that the Almighty God, creator of heaven and earth, wants to commune with you and me and is waiting for us to spend time with him. Jesus told the Samaritan woman at Jacob's well, *"Yet a time is coming and has now come when the true worshipers will worship the Father in spirit and truth, for they are the kind of worshipers the Father seeks"–John 4:23.*

We need to remember that God is waiting for us to meet with him in the morning or evening or whenever it works best for us. Everything else aside, this should motivate us for our quiet times with him.

One of the means of communication with God in our quiet time is the Bible.

Our quiet time should not only be a lesson preparation for the Sunday school class we are going to teach. Yes, God may want to give us something in our quiet time that we can use in our ministry, but it should not be our main focus to seek something specifically for that. We cannot really minister to others if we have neglected our own spiritual nourishment.

The objective we should have in our devotional time is to be fed spiritually, to be nourished by God's word. We should become more intimately acquainted with Jesus Christ, get to know more about what he has done for us, and discover what is on his heart and mind.

Set priorities

Make a plan, of how you can give God the fellowship He desires, and you receive your spiritual food. Pick a book of the Bible. Ask God to speak through the verses to you and make a commitment to do what you are told. The greatest profit we can have from our quiet time with God is to apply God's word to our life. Make notes. Ask yourself questions about the passage you are reading:

Prayer moves the Hand that moves the world

Some of the valuable principles I have learned in my relationship with God are:
When you want to be blessed, Give Him something you know He would want to bless.

When you want God to move on your behalf in what ever circumstance, give Him the room to move, and cooperate with that you see Him do.

When you want answers, read His Word, and seek His face. Pray in agreement with Him!

It was after our raising sheep experience that my wife and I were seeking God, for more direction in our lives that God opened a door for us to minister. Originally we wanted to go back to The Netherlands. However, while God kept that door closed, He opened another one, namely at the Teen Challenge Training Center in Rehrersburg, Pennsylvania. Having looked at different options, we received a phone call from Rev. Frank Reynolds, the Executive Director, who invited us to come as Counselor / Teacher. What included that we were to pastor / mentor / counsel / teach the students who were there, from being people with life controlling problems like substance abuse and with dysfunctional histories, to become a people who were whole and productive for the Lord.

For us that time was a very fruitful time, but also a time of further training in the ministry. It was a couple of years later still at this same training Center, that we felt a continuing pull to start a Teen Challenge, and were hoping to be able to do that in the Netherlands, but still, God kept that door firmly closed.

Somehow the thought and desire to start a Teen Challenge center remained pulling our hearth.

So we kept praying for an open door, so we could do that what we desired to do.

This went on until we received a phone call from the Executive Director from the state of Washington. He communicated to us that the Teen Challenge centers in this state were struggling to the point that they had to close down the residential center located in the heart of Seattle.

The only residential centers that had remained were the girl center, and the man's center in the Spokane area. He needed someone to come who knew and understood this ministry, and would be willing to try to turn it around. Seeing this as God's leading we ended up being the facility and area director of the Spokane Teen Challenge Training center.

Arriving there we had our work cut out for us, but we loved the challenge, until we became plagued by a number of bill collectors, who kept reminding me on a weekly basis that the bills were not paid, and unless we were going to pay before of the end of that month, we were not going to receive any service any more. Well I think you can understand, not having electricity, telephone, water and other supply's you mite as will close the doors, especially when you had six staff members and close to 20 students living at the same center. Those were times of great frustration. We had worked so hard to do every thing right. But still we had the feeling that we "were going two steps forwards, tree steps back." I had found out that we were in so much dept, that it was impossible to live up to the testimony we suppose to have as Christians. It came to the point that during one of my prayer walk, I started to pray," Lord, I know that you send us to this place, and we believe that we have been obedient to your Word, but lord I don't know anymore what to do. This ministry is not only representing my testimony, but also your testimony. So lord, you need to show me what to do. When you want this center to succeed, then please let it succeed. But when you want this place to die, please let it die, and let me know about it so I would not fight against you. But when you want this place to live, Show me the key?

During that prayer, God spoke to my heart, and gave me Matthew 18:18-20, where it says:

Verily I say unto you, whatsoever ye shall bind on earth shall be bound in heaven: and whatsoever ye shall loose on earth shall be loosed in heaven. Again I say unto you, That if two of you shall agree on earth as touching any thing that they shall ask, it shall be done for them of my Father which is in heaven. For where two or three are gathered together in my name, there am I in the midst of them.

The words," That if two of you shall agree on earth as touching any thing that they shall ask, it shall be done for them of my Father which is in heaven" kept echoing in my head when I read that. After this, coming back to my office, I started to write every need, every bill we had, on sheets of copy paper. One paper with the words, Electricity bill, and other telephone bill, until all the needs were written down. The next thing I did was taking those papers to the chapel, were I started to wall paper the walls with those needs. And when it was time for chapel, I explained the story to the staff and students who were present, and told them, that from that day forward, we were going to pray every weekday evening, from seven till eight. "In the spirit of agreement." "As touching any thing." From that time on things started to change. The bills started to get paid, and every need started to get med. Three and a halve year later, we came out of debt, and started to get some funds together designated for building improvement. We had a farm operation going with well over three hundred pigs, bringing in about two thousand dollars in the month. But most important, we saw students graduating on a monthly basis that did not just hear of God's faithfulness, but saw it happen right in front of them.

When God speaks to us through his word, we converse with him through prayer.

God has made him self accessible to us, yet so few believers avail themselves of the opportunity to talk with God. One of the reasons for this is that prayer is costly, and people who are not disciples are not willing to pay the price. It takes time and effort to converse with God through prayer. Everything in our world wars against prayer. Men who do not believe in God will not take time off for prayer. The devil does not want the people of God to pray. Our busy lives interfere with times of prayer. Rising early in the morning to pray is a challenge for many of us. Our body resists it; our mind resists it; and Satan resists it. But we must pray. It is our necessary lifeline to God.

When entering in, it is sometimes helpful to follow some practical principles.

Let me give you an example:

Acknowledge God for who He is, not only for what He can do.

Let's use the first words of the Lord's Prayer as our example.
"Our Father in heaven, hallowed be your name, your kingdom come, your will be done on earth as it is in heaven..."–Matthew 6:9-10

Confession.

The psalmist recognized the need for this and said, *"If I had cherished sin in my heart, the Lord would not have listened; but God has surely listened and heard my voice in prayer" (Psalm 66:18-19).*

The next step in praying is confession of all known sin to be sure the channel of communication is open. As we do this, we join David in asking God to look into our heart. *"Search me, 0 God, and know my heart; test me and know my anxious thoughts. See if there is any offensive way in me, and lead me in the way everlasting"–Psalm 139:23-24.*

As God searches our heart and places his finger on things that are displeasing to him, we confess our sins and ask him for forgiveness (1 John 1:9).

Solomon declared, *"He who conceals his sins does not prosper, but whoever confesses and renounces them finds mercy"-Proverbs 28:13.*

Praise.

After we have been cleansed, it is a good thing to continue our time of prayer with praise to God. You could play a worship tape and join in to help you focus on God. Praise expresses our adoration and our love for him. As we praise God, our thoughts should be focused on who he is, his greatness, power, majesty, love, grace, mercy, and longsuffering. You may want to use passages from his word that you have memorized. Many have found this to be extremely helpful in times of prayer. One of the most beautiful prayers of praise is that of David toward the end of his life (1 Chronicles 29:10-13).

Petition.

Finally, we need to pray for our self and our personal needs. (Philippians 4:6) Whatever these may be, we can bring them to God and expect him to answer. We should pray for specific things for which we expect specific answers. A great encouragement to me has been to think about my petitions in the past and see how God, miraculously has answered those prayers. As we pray in his will, according to his word, we have the assurance of Scripture that he will hear and answer.

Intercession.

We are responsible to pray for others. Many of us glibly promise to pray for people, but then we forget and do not intercede for them. One of the most helpful things we can do is to keep a prayer list on which we write down their names and requests. Then in our prayer time we can go over the list and pray for them specifically.

We should pray regularly for our pastors, Church leaders, Sunday school teachers, missionaries, and for our government. We should pray for those with whom we work, as well as for our family and friends who are close to us. We pray for others in the same way that we pray for ourselves, for our needs as human beings and as Christians are essentially the same. We can trust God to meet the needs of others as he does our own.

Be still, and know...

"Be still, and know that I am God"–Psalm 46:10.

We need to approach God in quietness.

Through Isaiah God said, *"In quietness and trust is your strength"–Isaiah 30:15.*

When our heart is still before him, he is able to speak to us through his word and give us that which we need for the day. If we are in a hurry, we may miss something of value. We must expect God to minister to us. God said: *"He who sacrifices thank offerings honors me, and he prepares the way so that I may show him the salvation of God."–Psalms 50:23.*

What simply means that when we respond to God with genuine love and adoration out of a pure heart, He then will respond back to us, in a way that will bless us.

Like wise, when we expose our life to God and invite him into the innermost parts of our heart, and when we concentrate on his word, we can expect the presence of God through his spirit. Anytime we expectantly read God's word, he will speak to us.

Thanksgiving.

The Apostle Paul wrote: *"Do not be anxious about anything, but in everything, by prayer and petition, with thanksgiving, present your requests to God. And the peace of God, which transcends all understanding, will guard your hearts and your minds in Christ Jesus." (Philippians 4:6,7)*

We need to learn to be a thankful people. Every day of our life we have something for which we can thank our Lord. We can thank him for our health, for his provision for all our needs, for safety, for the joyful times in our life, for friends, our church, and for the privilege of walking with Jesus Christ. You may want to sit down and make a list of all the things you ought to thank him for and then pray through the list. Remember to thank him for trials and difficult times as well, for they are intended for our benefit.

It is interesting to note that in the description of unsaved and rebellious people, Paul includes thanklessness. *"For although they knew God, they neither glorified him as God nor gave thanks to him, but their thinking became futile and their foolish hearts were darkened"* Romans 1:21.

We need to be aware of the danger of our quiet times becoming just something we do because of force of habit. Each meeting with God should be a time of anticipation because of our knowledge that he wants this fellowship with us and is waiting for us to come into his presence.

Each one of us is responsible to determine what time is best for us. Since most of us in our society have set times for our meals, why not a set time for something more important, our spiritual meals with God? The best way to guarantee that you will have your quiet time is to set aside a fixed time for that purpose. Many have chosen to set aside time in the morning. For some people it may be late in the evening when things have calmed down in their day. For others it might be a quiet time in the middle of the day when they can be alone. Decide what time best suits your schedule, and then stick to it. Make it a lordship commitment to God.

God wants us to have time with him. He invites us into his presence. He speaks to us through his word and we 'speak back to him through prayer. We must commit our self daily to this vital meeting with him.

10. The Attitude of a Servant

"This is how we know what love is: Jesus Christ laid down his life for us. And we ought to lay down our lives for our brothers" (1 John 3:16).

A disciple demonstrates a servant heart by helping others in practical ways. The Bible emphasizes serving others. A great example is that of Jesus as he washed the feet of his disciples. (John 13:3-17) He was a matchless demonstration of love and servant hood in that he came to die for the sins of men.

When God spoke to our heart to go to the United States, God gave me a vision of what I was going to be doing there when I arrived. However I had no clue how to start or even approach this. So when we ended up in the U.SA., I could only do that what I knew I could do, which was evangelizing the streets, find work somewhere so we could pay the bills, and plug ourselves in to the church. It was about three months later that we saw God unfold that what God showed me I would be doing. The church we had become a part of was the church that had supported JoAnne on her mission's adventure. It was an affiliate Four Square Church, and it had at that time two co-pastors and seven elders. After one of the church services one of the pastors came to us, and said that they wanted to talk to us at one of their counsel meetings. It was while attending this meeting the puzzle peaces came together. They said, "Why didn't you tell us that God had send you here as a missionary"? God had spoken to them that they needed to invite me to be more involved in the church as well with the Christian school which was one of the ministries of the church. However, in order to make it all possible I would have to work as a custodian, keeping the building including the bathrooms clean. At the same time I could improve my English, as my native language was Dutch, and by working at the church, cleaning, and teaching practical evangelism and discipleship to the students, I would be able to build and strengthen the relationships I needed to be able to minister to them. One of the things I learned through this was that servant hood was the vehicle to a greater ministry. Working at the church and the school, doing physical ministry, opened the door to a lot of spiritual ministry.

Much later, speaking at a Bible Seminary, not knowing the students, I once asked them the question, why they were there, and how many of them had plans to become a pastor, a teacher, an evangelist or missionary? When nobody responded, I was puzzled, so I asked them what their plans were when they finished this school. They then responded by, "We are called to be prophets!"

Personally, I believe that the offices and gifts of the Holy Spirit are still as valid today, as they were 2000 years ago, however we can not exclude them from being a servant first.

The Christian emphasis on servant hood is contrary to the practice of most secular leadership. In most cases those in high management demand service from others. It seems that's the way things are done in our world. But when Jesus came, he reversed the direction of service without giving up his leadership. In fact he enhanced his leadership because of his service. Jesus taught the disciples to be servants.

During a discussion on who should be the greatest, he told them: *"You know that the rulers of the Gentiles lord it over them, and their high officials exercise authority over them. Not so with you. Instead, whoever wants to become great among you must be your servant, and whoever wants to be first must be your slave—just as the Son of Man did not come to be served, but to serve, and to give his life as a ransom for many."*– Matthew 20:25-28.

This teaching of leadership by serving continues to have an unfamiliar ring in an age that calls for us to do everything we can to climb to the top. The Bible teaches that to lead is to serve. We may recognize the truth of this concept and respond with a positive attitude. The problem, however, arises in doing it day to day.

Since servant hood is taught in the Bible as part of being a disciple of Jesus Christ, we want to examine what a servant is, look at some characteristics of a servant, and discover how we can be servants practically. The chapter concludes with a few thoughts about the blessings of a life of servant hood.

What is a servant?

Paul introduced himself to the church in Rome as a servant first, then an apostle.
"Paul, a servant of Christ Jesus, called to be an apostle and set apart for the gospel of God...–Romans 1:1.
Apostleship was an office, but servant hood deals with people. One of the greatest honors that anyone could grant us would be to call us a servant of Christ. Throughout the history of the church, godly men and women have often been designated by expressions such as "a true servant of the Lord."

Jesus gave us the basic summary of his life:
"For even the Son of man came not to be ministered unto, but to minister and to give his life a ransom for many"–Mark 10:45.

He was among us as one who served.
For who is greater, the one who is at the table or the one who serves? Is it not the one who is at the table? But I am among you as one who serves.–Luke 22:27.

To serve God we must serve others, as Jesus did.

Be imitators of God, therefore, as dearly loved children and live a life of love, just as Christ loved us and gave himself up for us as a fragrant offering and sacrifice to God–Ephesians 5:1-2

The leader must offer his own life on the altar of God to be consumed in the flame of God's love, in service to others. The term servant, according to the Scriptures, cannot easily be tied down to one specific definition. Rather, it is used to mean a variety of things.

Many times a servant is also called a slave.

The Hebrews in the Old Testament had two types of servants or slaves, those bought and those taken in wars. In that society people were also able to sell themselves to pay their debts. In the Bible entire nations were required to serve their king or those who conquered them. So Israel is spoken of as a servant to her king and the Syrians are referred to as the servants of King David. Depending on the course of history, the Israelites served the Philistines, and on other occasions the Philistines served Israel.

The person who dedicates himself to the service of another by his own choice of will is also considered a servant. So we find that Joshua became the servant of Moses, Elisha became the servant of Elijah, and the disciples became servants of Christ.

"For we do not preach ourselves, but Jesus Christ as Lord, and ourselves as your servants for Jesus' sake"–(2 Corinthians 4:5).

The Apostle Paul chose to be a servant. *"Though I am free and belong to no man, I make myself a slave to everyone, to win as many as possible"– 1 Corinthians 9:19.* In all of these cases these men were eventually exalted to higher positions.

"Thanks be to God that, though you used to be slaves to sin, you wholeheartedly obeyed the form of teaching to which you were entrusted. You have been set free from sin and have become slaves to righteousness."–Romans 6:17-18).

A person who serves God in a particular function or calling is designated a servant of God. Jesus Christ, for example, is called God's servant prophetically (see Isaiah 53:11).

The expression "servant of God" may be applied to a person whom God uses to perform his will in a particular mercy or judgment.

Moses, for example, is called the servant of God seventeen times in the Scriptures, and David is so designated some twenty-four times.

Putting these biblical teachings together, we discover that a servant is a person who doesn't exercise his own will but rather submits it in order to please his master. He also demonstrates the importance of serving another without any assurance of reward.

Let's identify some of the important Biblical characteristics of a servant:

He is filled with the Holy Spirit.

On the Day of Pentecost, Peter declared that Joel's prophecy was fulfilled and the age of the Holy Spirit had come. *"This is what was spoken by the prophet Joel:... 'Even on my servants, both men and women, I will pour out my Spirit in those days'"–Acts 2:16, 18.*

The power and filling of the Holy Spirit of God are necessary for real servant hood. Without Him we can't do anything. (John 15:4-5)

He is motivated by love.

He knows that he is serving Jesus. The Apostle Paul encourages us saying, *"And whatever you do, do it heartily, as to the Lord and not to men."– Colossians 3:23*

"For you, brethren, have been called to liberty; only do not use liberty as an opportunity for the flesh, but through love serve one another."– Galatians 5:13

Jesus said, *"I say to you, inasmuch as you did it to one of the least of these My brethren, you did it to Me."–Matthew 25:40*

He is patient.

Paul urged Timothy, as a servant, to be patient (see 2 Timothy 2:24, KJV). One of the results of impatience is discouragement. A servant should do his work and not become discouraged when things don't go his way.

He is gentle.

"Those who oppose him he must gently instruct, in the hope that God will grant them repentance leading them to acknowledge the truth" (2 Timothy 2:25). Paul instructed Timothy to be gentle with those of the opposition whom he would be instructing in the things of God.

He serves in an attitude of humility.

He does not attract attention to himself. He stays in the background and does his work. Jesus taught that "a student is not above his teacher, nor a servant above his master"–Matthew 10:24.

He is faithfully doing his work.

Some of Jesus' strongest words were directed to this area of serving. *"Who then is the faithful and wise servant, whom the master has put in charge of the servants in his household to give them their food at the proper time? It will be good for that servant whose master finds him doing so when he returns. I tell you the truth, he will put him in charge of all his possessions–Matthew 24:45-47.*

Jesus taught on one occasion. Suppose one of you had a servant plowing or looking after the sheep. Would he say to the servant when he comes in from the field, *"Come along now and sit down to eat"? Would he not rather say, "Prepare my supper, get your self ready and wait on me while I eat and drink; after that you may eat and drink"?–Luke 17:7-8.*

He is able to teach.

Primarily this means able to teach others to be servants. This is another characteristic that Paul urged as he challenged Timothy to serve others. *"And the Lord's servant must not quarrel; instead, he must be kind to everyone, able to teach, not resentful"–2 Timothy 2:24.*
.In countries where people work as servants, the older servants teach the younger everything they know about service to their masters.

He is obedient.

Paul wrote: *"Slaves, obey your earthly masters with respect and fear, and with sincerity of heart, just as you would obey Christ. Obey them not only to win their favor when their eye is on you, but like slaves of Christ, doing the will of God from your heart"–Ephesians 6:5-6.*

One of the responsibilities of Christian leadership is to *"teach slaves to be subject to their masters in everything, to try to please them, not to talk back to them"-(Titus 2:9.*

He is dedicated.

When a servant commits himself to the one whom he serves, he does it with the totality of his heart. Just look at Elisha; Then Elijah said to him, "Stay here, Elisha; the LORD has sent me to Jericho." And he replied, *"As surely as the LORD lives and as you live, I will not leave you."–2 Kings 2:4.*

We have another beautiful example of that in Ittai the Gittite. David had been ousted in a palace coup by his son Absalom, and was now fleeing for his life. Ittai had gone with him, but David tried to convince him to return to King Absalom. "But Ittai replied to the king, *"As surely as the Lord lives, and as my lord the king lives, wherever my lord the king may be, whether it means life or death, there will your servant be "–2 Samuel 15:21.*

He is alert to the needs of his master.

Jesus spoke often about watchfulness. *"Be dressed ready for service and keep your lamps burning, like men waiting for their master to return from a wedding banquet, so that when he comes and knocks they can immediately open the door for him"–Luke 12:35-36.*

How to be a servant;

Here are some suggestions on how we can be servants of Jesus Christ and others.

Be Willing to Do Menial Tasks

This is one of the hardest things to teach to a person in Western society today. Many think that menial tasks are below them. Note this incident in the life of the Apostle Paul: Once safely on shore, we found out that the island was called Malta. The islanders showed us unusual kindness. They built a fire and welcomed us all because it was raining and cold. Paul gathered a pile of brushwood and, as he put it on the fire, a viper, driven out by the heat, fastened itself on his hand (Acts 28:1-3).

Notice this; the great Apostle Paul gathered firewood on a cold, rainy day right after a traumatic shipwreck. He could just as easily have rested and let the kind islanders do all the work. But Paul was a servant and demonstrated it vividly even at the expense of being bitten by a snake. Possibly that opened up an opportunity to proclaim the gospel.

Be Available

One of the characteristics of servants in a household is that they must be available when the master calls them. The Christian servant must also be available to God and to those it is his ministry to serve.

We must not be like those who made all kinds of excuses when Jesus called them to follow him. He said to another man, *"Follow me."* But the man replied, *"Lord, first let me go and bury my father."* Jesus said to him, *"Let the dead bury their own dead, but you go and proclaim the kingdom of God."* Still another said, *"I will follow you, Lord; but first let me go back and say good-by to my family."* Jesus replied, *" No one who puts his hand to the plow and looks back is fit for service in the kingdom of God"*–Luke 9:59-62.

Be Observant

A servant must be alert to the needs of others. The psalmist wrote, *"As the eyes of slaves look to the hand of their master, as the eyes of a maid look to the hand of her mistress, so our eyes look to the Lord our God, till he shows us his mercy"*–Psalm 123:2. The needs of guests in a Hebrew household were communicated to the servants by hand signals, so it was the responsibility of those serving to watch the hands of the master and mistress.

Go the second mile

If someone forces you to go one mile, go with him two miles.–Matthew 5:41

Western society is governed by clock-watching. People do just what they are asked to do, nothing more. If they are asked to do a little more than their job description calls for, they want overtime or other compensation. A true servant does what he is supposed to do, and more.

What happens in a person's life when he manifests the characteristics of servant hood? The Bible does have something to say about these "rewards." The servant may experience the service of his master. *"It will be good for those servants whose master finds them watching when he comes. I tell you the truth, he will dress himself to serve, will have them recline at the table and will come and wait on them. It will be good for those servants whose master finds them ready, even if he comes in the second or third watch of the night–Luke 12:37-38.*

The servant who is faithful in all his responsibilities will be recognized by the master whom he so faithfully serves. The master of such a man will say, *"Well done, good and faithful servant! You have been faithful with a few things; I will put you in charge of many things. Come and share your master's happiness!"–Matthew 25:21.*

God gives his servants wisdom for the responsibilities committed to them.
When Solomon became king, he prayed: *"Your servant is here among the people you have chosen, a great people, too numerous to count or number. So give your servant a discerning heart to govern your people and to distinguish between right and wrong. For who is able to govern this great people of yours?–1 Kings 3:8-9.*
God granted his request for wisdom, and Solomon became one of the wisest men who ever lived.
Honor from God comes to the faithful servant of the Lord. Jesus said, *"Whoever serves me must follow me; and where I am, my servant also will be. My Father will honor the one who serves me"–John 12:26.* You cannot be a true disciple of Jesus Christ unless you have a servant heart.

11. The Ministry of Giving

As you go, preach this message: 'The kingdom of heaven is near. 'Heal the sick, raise the dead, and cleanse those who have leprosy, drive out demons. Freely you have received, freely give.–Matthew 10:7-8

Throughout the Bible Jesus wants us to be givers not just receivers.

He encourages us to give love to friends and enemies (without discrimination);

to give mercy to those in need; to give forgiveness to those who mistreated us; to give encouragement to everyone, and praise where it is deserved; to live in a way that it could be an inspiration to others.

An example can be found in Acts 3:6, where Peter said, *"Silver or gold I do not have, but what I have I give you. In the name of Jesus Christ of Nazareth, walk."* Jesus encourages us to give to others, as if we were giving to Him.

He said, *"I tell you the truth, whatever you did for one of the least of these brethren of mine, you did it for me.–Matt. 25:40*

But one other very important way of giving, is from our finances.

One of the great privileges that we have in our Christian life is giving to God's work. Giving is a lordship decision, in which we turn over control of our possessions to Christ. Giving also is an evidence of our gratitude for what he has done for us.

Biblical principles of giving

"Do not store up for yourselves treasures on earth, where moth and rust destroy, and where thieves break in and steal. But store up for yourselves treasures in heaven, where moth and rust do not destroy, and where thieves do not break in and steal" (Matthew 6:19-20).

Jesus said in the Sermon on the Mount: that we invest our treasures in heaven by giving to the poor of this world. "Jesus looked at him [the rich young man] and loved him. *'One thing you lack,' he said. 'Go, sell everything you have and give to the poor, and you will have treasure in heaven. Then come, follow me"–Mark 10:21*. This man had so much, yet he lacked treasure in heaven.

Paul wrote to a very generous church and said, *"Not that I am looking for a gift, but I am looking for what may be credited to your account" Philippians 4:17*.

The context of this statement tells of the generosity of the Philippians in supporting Paul, in sharing with him out of their poverty, and in sending him aid when he had needs. Whatever we give will be credited to our spiritual account. God will not forget our genuine works of love. We may not be recognized by men in this world, nor receive monetary rewards, but God will never forget what we have done for him.

"God is not unjust; he will not forget your work and the love you have shown him as you have helped his people and continue to help them"– Hebrews 6:10.

The psalmist wrote:
The man who fears the Lord "*has scattered abroad his gifts to the poor, his righteousness endures for ever"–Psalm 112:9*.

This is not our righteousness in terms of sin, but our acting rightly in terms of giving. Treasures in heaven result from helping the people of God. This principle is supported by Solomon. *"He who is kind to the poor lends to the Lord, and he will reward him for what he has done"–Proverbs 19:17*.

Tithing

"I the LORD do not change. So you, O descendants of Jacob, are not destroyed. Ever since the time of your forefathers you have turned away from my decrees and have not kept them. Return to me, and I will return

to you," says the LORD Almighty. "But you ask, 'How are we to return?' "Will a man rob God? Yet you rob me. "But you ask, 'How do we rob you?' "In tithes and offerings. You are under a curse—the whole nation of you—because you are robbing me. Bring the whole tithe into the storehouse, that there may be food in my house. Test me in this," says the LORD Almighty, "and see if I will not throw open the floodgates of heaven and pour out so much blessing that you will not have room enough for it. I will prevent pests from devouring your crops, and the vines in your fields will not cast their fruit," says the LORD Almighty. "Then all the nations will call you blessed, for yours will be a delightful land," says the LORD Almighty.–Malachi 3:6-12

Before God send us to the United States, to work as a missionary, I was taught that we were New Testament people. We were free from the law. We were still encouraged that we gave when the Spirit moved us to do so. But being free from the law meant that we did not have to pay our tithes any more. Of course you can understand that that was the lifestyle I had adopted for myself. I gave when I felt like it. It was when I came to the USA that my position started to change.

Having arrived on my new mission field, believing that God had send us, and that He would take care of us, I started to Evangelize while doing some odd jobs here in there—from cutting rhubarb, picking apples, or bringing bales of hay from the field into the barn. My wife had found an office job not far away from where we lived. At the same we were praying that God would provide us with the needs we had. Things like a vacuum cleaner, a washing machine, a wash dryer, a car, money for a telephone and for car insurance just in case God was going to bless us by providing one.

While doing what we could do, and praying for God's provision God started to speak to me through His Word. He said, "Give me your *tithe." First I could not believe what God asked me to do. I asked my self, "Giving my tithe of what?" We could hardly pay the bills we had. We could not afford it! But God was patient with me, and kept repeating to me about the need for me to pay Him my tithes. When finally talking it over with my wife we decided to take this step of faith and on a weekly basis started to give God our tithes.

(* Tithing is giving to God 10+ percent of your gross income. It is a

form of giving back to God a part of the blessings you received from Him. They are an expression of both love and trust for God, as the Lord promised to bless the works of His people's hands [Deuteronomy 14:29])

Note what happened next. It was about five weeks later that things started to happen. It was one miracle after the other. In a period of two weeks God blessed us with ALL the things we had prayed for and more. The value of all those things together was bigger then all the money my wife and I had earned together. I believe it is needless to say that I changed my beliefs and behavior. Yes, we are free from that law, stating that we have to tithe, but I do believe that when you love God, and place your trust in Him, you would want too.

"Bring the whole tithe into the storehouse, that there may be food in my house. Test me in this, and see if I will not throw open the floodgates of heaven and pour out so much blessing that you will not have room enough for it"–Malachi 3:10.

God promised to provide

On a number of occasions God has shown us that he cannot be out given. He gives back far more than is ever given to him. In fact, He pours it out on those who give generously. The prophet recorded God's words in the Old Testament:

Solomon referred more than once to God's abundant supply. *"One man gives freely, yet gains even more; another withholds unduly, but comes to poverty. A generous man will prosper; he who refreshes others will himself be refreshed"–Proverbs 11:24-25.*

In the *King James Version* the phrase *will prosper* is translated "shall be made fat," a vivid picture of God's blessing on liberality.

Earlier Solomon had advised God's people to *"honor the Lord with your wealth, with the first fruits of all your crops; then your barns will be filled to overflowing, and your vats will brim over with new wine"–Proverbs 3:9-10.*

In our day and age this simply means that God will provide more than we need, even as he did in the agricultural society of ancient Israel. We may also receive blessings of another kind. Because the early Church gave so freely to one another, they experienced unity, love, gladness, singleness of heart, praise, and growth in numbers (Acts 2:44-47).

The Apostle Paul wrote:
"My God will meet all your needs according to his glorious riches in Christ Jesus" (Philippians 4:19).
Whatever our needs may be, spiritual, physical, or financial, God promises to meet them. Paul thanked one church for their ample gifts and concluded with the assurance that 'The implication is that if we give of our substance, God will supply all our needs.

Jesus talking about an important principle of giving said:
"Give and it will be given to you. A good measure, pressed down, shaken together and running over, will be poured into your lap. For with the measure you use, it will be measured to you" (Luke 6:38).

God desires to give us blessings beyond simply meeting our needs. Paul he stated that *"whoever sows sparingly will also reap sparingly, and whoever sows generously will also reap generously"–2 Corinthians 9:6.*

We cannot determine of what form God's blessing will have, but we can determine the quantity by how much we have given.

One of the reasons some Christians continue to be plagued with financial troubles is because of their own giving. If a Christian is not honoring God with his income, he will experience financial difficulties.

Let's have a closer look at some other Biblical principles on how we are to give to the Lord and to his work.

We are to give willingly, cheerfully and joyfully.

Each man should give what he has decided in his heart to give, not reluctantly or under compulsion, for God loves a cheerful giver (2 Corinthians 9:7).

Giving is never to be done with a grudging attitude or as the result of pressure. We have already seen that in the days of David the *people "had given freely and whole-heartedly to the Lord"–1 Chronicles 29:9.*

In his prayer later on, David added: *"I know, my God, that you test the heart and are pleased with integrity. All these things have I given willingly and with honest intent. And now I have seen with joy how willingly your people who are here have given to you"–1 Chronicles 29:17.*

Paul taught this principle in the New Testament.

"For if the willingness is there, the gift is acceptable according to what one has, not according to what he does not have"–2 Corinthians 8:12

He goes on to say that *"each man should give what he has decided in his heart to give, not reluctantly or under compulsion, for God loves a cheerful giver"–2 Corinthians 9:7.*

We should consider giving such a privilege that joy should well up in our hearts because we are able to do so. The church at Philippi was known for its joyful giving. *"And now, brothers, we want you to know about the grace that God has given the Macedonian churches [Philippi among them]. Out of the most severe trial, their overflowing joy and their extreme poverty welled up in rich generosity"–2 Corinthians 8:1-2.*

We give because we are merciful to those in need. That was the attitude of the psalmist when he wrote, *"The wicked borrows, and cannot pay back, but the righteous is generous and gives"*–Psalm 37:21.

Paul urged his readers to *"share with God's people who are in need"*– Romans 12:13.

He explained this to the Corinthians: Our desire is not that others might be relieved while you are hard pressed, but that there might be equality. At the present time your plenty will supply what they need, so that in turn their plenty will supply what you need. Then there will be equality, as it is written: *"He that gathered much did not have too much and he that gathered little did not have too little"–2 Corinthians 8:13-15.*

We are to give generously and sacrificially.

In many passages which we have looked at already, the Bible urges generosity. When Paul was talking about spiritual gifts, he said of giving, *"If it is contributing to the needs of others, let him give generously"*–Romans 12:8.

The Macedonian churches were known for their sacrificial giving (see 2 Corinthians 8:2-3). The most beautiful example of that kind of giving is the observation of Jesus one day in the temple. As he looked up, Jesus saw the rich putting their gifts into the temple treasury. He also saw a poor widow put in two very small copper coins. *"I tell you the truth,"* he said, *"this poor widow has put in more than all the others. All these people gave their gifts out of their wealth; but she out of her poverty put in all she had to live on"*–Luke 21:1-4.

Jesus talks about giving without seeking recognition or earthly rewards.

This does not necessarily mean anonymously, but it does mean that we do not seek the recognition of our giving from others. He taught this in the Sermon on the Mount:

"Be careful not to do your "acts of righteousness" before men, to be seen by them. If you do, you will have no reward from your Father in heaven... But when you give to the needy, do not let your left hand know what your right hand is doing, so that your giving may be in secret. Then you're Father, who sees what is done in secret, will reward you–Matthew 6:1, 3-4.

Give as unto the Lord

He will put the sheep on his right and the goats on his left. "Then the King will say to those on his right, 'Come, you who are blessed by my Father; take your inheritance, the kingdom prepared for you since the creation of the world. For I was hungry and you gave me something to eat, I was thirsty and you gave me something to drink, I was a stranger and you invited me in, I needed clothes and you clothed me, I was sick and you looked after me, I was in prison and you came to visit me.' "Then the righteous will answer him, 'Lord, when did we see you hungry and feed you, or thirsty and give you something to drink? When did we see you a stranger and invite you in, or needing clothes and clothe you? When did we see you sick or in prison and go to visit you?' "The King will reply, 'I tell you the truth, whatever you did for one of the least of these brothers of mine, you did for me.' "Then he will say to those on his left, 'Depart from me, you who are cursed, into the eternal fire prepared for the devil and his angels. For I was hungry and you gave me nothing to eat, I was thirsty and you gave me nothing to drink, I was a stranger and you did not invite me in, I needed clothes and you did not clothe me, I was sick and in prison and you did not look after me.' "They also will answer, 'Lord, when did we see you hungry or thirsty or a stranger or needing clothes or sick or in prison, and did not help you?' "He will reply, 'I tell you the truth, whatever you did not do for one of the least of these, you did not do for me.'–Matthew 25:33-45

Benevolence giving

"Suppose a brother or sister is without clothes and daily food. If one of you says to him, 'Go, I wish you well; keep warm and well fed,' but does nothing about his physical needs, what good is it?"–James 2:15-16

God wants us to give to practical, and the physical needs. Paul exhorted the former thief, a person who had now come to Christ, to make giving to the needy an integral part of his life. *"He who has been stealing must steal no longer, but must work, doing something useful with his own hands, that he may have something to share with those in need"–Ephesians 4:28.*

The needy are all around us, including in our churches.

Throughout Scripture the people of God are called on to support those who work for the Lord full-time. In the Old Testament nation of Israel, the people were reminded that they had to support the Levites. They were men of the tribe of Levi who were serving the Lord in the tabernacle and as instructors of the Law. Moses wrote, *"Be careful not to neglect the Levites as long as you live in your land"–Deuteronomy 12:19.*

The people were responsible to take care of the needs of these religious workers.

Supporting those in full time ministry

Many ministers and missionaries are because of their constant traveling not able to hold a job and receiving a monthly salary. They are in need of support from others who believe in their ministry, and want to partner with them.

We find a beautiful example of that in the gospels as Jesus was proclaiming the good news. The Twelve were traveling with him, as were some women who had been cured of evil spirits and diseases.

"These women were helping to support them out of their own means"– *Luke 8:3.*

We are to support those who instruct us. Paul told the Galatians,

"Anyone who receives instruction in the word must share all good things with his instructor.–Galatians 6:6.

Epaphroditus is an example of a person supporting and ministering to another. Paul wrote of him, *"But I think it is necessary to send back to you Epaphroditus, my brother, fellow worker and fellow soldier, who is also your messenger, whom you sent to take care of my needs"*–Philippians 2:25. He ministered to Paul's needs in many ways.

The starting point in our giving must be the local church in which we are being ministered to with the word of God. We are also responsible to give to foreign missions organizations, or individual missionaries. Each of these groups has the need of the support from individuals who are willing to stand with them, support them, and pray for them so that they can focus completely on the ministry they are called to fulfill.

Give to the Lord First

The Bible's presentation of giving is that we should give to the Lord first, as Paul suggested. *"On the first day of every week, each one of you should set aside a sum of money in keeping with his income, saving it up, so that when I come no collections will have to be made"*–1 Corinthians 16:2).

This does not mean that we have to give every week, but we are to be regular in our giving. If you are paid twice a month, you might want to give twice a month; if you have structured your giving at the end of the month, give at the end of the month. The main point is to be consistent in your giving. This is what Paul taught the Corinthians in the passage above.

"It is more blessed to give than to receive"–Acts 20:35.

Special needs will arise periodically, and it is our privilege to give extra gifts to meet those needs. This is part of our opportunity to be generous with what the Lord has prospered us. Remember, God can never be out given!

Honor Your Pledges

"Let your 'Yes' be 'Yes,' and your 'No,' 'No' "–Matthew 5:37

It is as with everything else in your Christian life, when you make a commitment or pledge, be sure that you can, and will fulfill it. Determine with God's help what you can do. Never make a pledge that would take money away from your local church commitment.

If the level of your income falls and you are unable to meet your commitments on a regular basis, be sure to notify the church, organization, or individual. It is simply a courtesy to them and helps them in their planning and raising of further support. I know how we have appreciated being notified by people when they had to cut down or were not able to financially support us any longer.

Giving is a privilege and an honor for Christian disciples. According to the teachings of God's Word, he will bless what we give joyfully and ungrudgingly to him and his workers. We are storing up treasure in heaven which will be a part of that great reward when we stand before Jesus Christ.

12. Your Personal Project

Then Jesus came to them and said, "All authority in heaven and on earth has been given to me. Therefore go and make disciples of all nations, baptizing them in the name of the Father and of the Son and of the Holy Spirit, and teaching them to obey everything I have commanded you. And surely I am with you always, to the very end of the age."– Matthew 28:18-20

As you have read this book, I want to encourage you to:

Prayerfully read the following Bible verses over again.
Allow the verses to sink in, and allow them to relate to you.

Make personal notes of what these verses say to you, and what they could mean to you.

Prayerfully consider the question of how you can implement these verses into your live.

Ask God to help you, to align yourself with His plan and purpose.

Try to memorize at least one Bible verse out of each chapter of the book. Meditated on them, and recall them when difficult situations arise.

Thank Him for all the blessings He bestowed upon you.

Look for opportunities to share with others from some of the many blessings you have received yourself.

Jesus said, "If you hold to my teaching, you are really my disciples.– John 8:31

Conclusion

This book was written to tell you about God's love, His mercy and His saving grace.

To encourage those who feel lost and are looking for answers, and for those who need a revelation of their purpose in live.

To exhort those who are confessing to be Christians, and to empower those who want to be actively involved in encouraging and mentoring others—Making Disciples.

To use a Dutch saying, *"When you want to change the world, you need to start with your self."*

Disciple making begins with you. You have to be a disciple before you can make another disciple. There will be struggles and difficulties. You will discover it is costly. But the Holy Spirit will help you through with the end result that you become the person planed for you to be.

Your personal desire to become a man of God or a woman of God must have priority, for it is from this platform of living example that you can launch out to reach and train others. In fact, when people see your life, they will be motivated to come to you seeking your spiritual assistance. And remember, the vitality of your relationship to Christ is very important in a disciple making ministry.

Start today by asking God to bring a person into your life to disciple, and begin to look for that person. You won't be making disciples tomorrow if you don't get started today.

My Closing Thoughts

Not that I have already obtained all this, or have already been made perfect, but I press on to take hold of that for which Christ Jesus took hold of me. Brothers, I do not consider myself yet to have taken hold of it. But one thing I do: Forgetting what is behind and straining toward what is ahead, I press on toward the goal to win the prize for which God has called me heavenward in Christ Jesus. All of us who are mature should take such a view of things. And if on some point you think differently, that too God will make clear to you. Only let us live up to what we have already attained. Join with others in following my example, brothers, and take note of those who live according to the pattern we gave you. For, as I have often told you before and now say again even with tears, many live as enemies of the cross of Christ. Their destiny is destruction, their god is their stomach, and their glory is in their shame. Their mind is on earthly things. But our citizenship is in heaven. And we eagerly await a Savior from there, the Lord Jesus Christ, who, by the power that enables him to bring everything under his control, will transform our lowly bodies so that they will be like his glorious body.–Philippians 3:12-21

Scripture Index

God's plan from the beginning:

Jeremiah 1:4-10
Jeremiah 29:11-14
John 15:16
1 Peter 2:9
John 17:4-23
Ephesians 2:10
Romans 11:27-29
John 10:10
Genesis 30:22–50:26
Eph 3:20, 21
Matthew 28:18-20
Luke 14:25-27, 33
2 Corinthians 5:17-20

A changed life

Ephesians 4:17, 18
Isaiah 6:5
Acts 2:28-41
Psalm 66:18
Romans 6:19
2 Corinthians 6:17
John 11:17-44
1 John 1:7-10
Romans 12:1, 2
Philippians 4:8

Ephesians 2:8, 9
Colossians 3:2
Luke 9:62
Philippians 2:12-14
1 Peter 1:14-16
Proverbs 8:13
2 Timothy 3:1-5
1 Peter 1:13-17
1 Peter 1:22-23
2 Corinthians 7:1
Galatians 5:16-25
Ephesians 4:30
2 Peter 1:3-9
1 Corinthians 6:19-20
1 Thessalonians 4:3-5
2 Corinthians 10:4-5
Job 31:1
Ephesians 5:4
Ephesians 4:25-32
Proverbs 18:24
Proverbs 27:17
1 Peter 2:11-12
2 Timothy 2:22
1 Peter 5:8
Ephesians 6:12, 13
Romans 16:19, 20
1 Corinthians 10:13
Titus 2:11-14
Romans 8:13, 14

Being Teachable

Matthew 11:28-30
Luke 6:40
Philippians 4:9
1 Thessalonians 1:6, 7

1 Corinthians 11:1
John 13:35
2 Corinthians 3:18
Galatians 5:22-23
2 Timothy 2:20-21
1 Corinthians 6:19-20
Luke 7:44-48
Matthew 6:14-15
Luke 23:34
Mark 7:37
Luke 16:10
2 Corinthians 2:12-13
Colossians 3:23-24
Hebrews 11:6
Hebrews 11:24-25
Hebrews 11:13
Galatians 6:7-10
Ephesians 1:17
Matthew 6:33
Philippians 4:4-9
1 Corinthians 15:58
Romans 4:20-21
John 14:6
John 3:14-17
James 1:18
1 Peter 1:23
Romans 15:4
Psalms 119:155
Hebrews 4:12
Psalm 119:9-11
Hebrews 5:12
1 Peter 2:2-3
Acts 20:32
Proverbs 3:5-6
Psalm 37:4-5
2 Corinthians 5:19-20

Ezekiel 2:4
Acts 22:14-15
Proverbs 22:20-21
2 Timothy 3:16-17
Matthew 7:13-14
Jeremiah 9:23-24
Romans 10:17
James 1:22-25
Deuteronomy 17:19
Revelation 1:3
1 Timothy 4:13
Proverbs 2:1-4
2 Timothy 2:15
Acts 17:11
Colossians 3:16
Deuteronomy 6:6
Proverbs 7:2-3
Philippians 2:5
Psalm 119:11
John 14:21
1 Peter 2:2
Psalm 32:8
John 15:7
John 16:24
1 John 5:14-15
Philippians 4:9
1 Peter 3:15
Isaiah 50:4
Psalm 1:1-3

Filled with the Holy Spirit

Acts 1:4-5
Hebrews 13:8
Exodus 3:14
John 14:15-18

Luke 11:9-13
1 Timothy 3:16
Genesis 1:1
1 Corinthians 2:10-11
1 Corinthians 12:11
Romans 8:27
Romans 15:30
John 15:26, 16:13
John 1:16-17
John 16:7-15
John 14:16
Acts 13:2
Romans 8:26
1 John 2:20, 27
John 14:26
Acts 16:6-7
Genesis 6:3
Ephesians 4:30
Hebrews 10:29
Acts 5:3
Matthew 12:31-32
Matthew 28:19
2 Corinthians 13:14
Acts 15:28
John 14:26
1 John 2:27
1 Corinthians 2:13-14
2 Corinthians 4:18
John 14:26
John 16:12-13
2 Peter 1:3
Acts 1:4-5
Joel 2:28
Acts 1:8
Zechariah 4:6
John 15:4-5

KNOWN BEFORE BIRTH

Romans 7:15-25
Galatians 5:17-18
Matthew 26:41
Hebrews 11:1, 6
1 Corinthians 11:17-34
Matthew 28:20
Mark 16:20
Mark 14:27-31, 53, 72
Acts 4:5, 23-31
Philippians 1:4-6
1 Corinthians 13
1 Corinthians 12:1-7
Romans 12:5-6
Philippians 2:13
1 Peter 4:10
Romans 12:3-8
Romans 2:1-3
1 Peter 4:10
1 Corinthians 14:1
Galatians 5:13
Colossians 3:23-24
Colossians 3:16
Matthew 28:20
Hebrews 3:13
Hebrews 10:25
Matthew 10:3
Luke 6:38
Romans 12:13
1 Timothy 3:4
Proverbs 17:2
Proverbs 16:32
Luke 10:37
2 Corinthians 13:8
Colossians 3:12
Galatians 5:22-23
Acts 19:18-19

Acts 5:41-42
Acts 2:47
2 Timothy 2:6
Ephesians 4:30
James 3:9-12
1 Samuel 15:23
1 Corinthians 11:1
2 Peter 3:18
1 Peter 2:20-21
Romans 8:29
Romans 13:14
2 Peter 1:5-8
Acts 19:1-6
John 3:14-16
Acts 2:38-39
Romans 8:9
Matthew 6:33
Luke 22:42
Luke 11:11
Galatians 3:2
James 1:6-8
Romans 12:1-2
James 4:3
Acts 5:32
1 Peter 4:1-2, 10

Sharing your faith

Acts 1:8
1 Peter 3:15-16
Titus 2:14
Luke 24
Acts 2:42-47
Acts 19:1-20
Acts 5:42
Acts 4:13

KNOWN BEFORE BIRTH

Acts 11:19, 21
Matthew 12:30
Acts 26:4-5, 9-11, 19-23
Acts 4:13-14, 29, 31
Romans 3:10-18, 23
Romans 5:12, 6:23
Hebrews 9:27
Exodus 34:6-7
Romans 5:8
Isaiah 53:6
1 Peter 2:24
Ephesians 2:8-9
Titus 3:5
Romans 3:24
Proverbs 28:13
1 John 1:9
Revelations 3:20
John 1:12
Romans 10:9-10
John 5:24
1 John 5:11-13
John 10:28
Hebrews 7:25
1 Timothy 1:12
Zechariah 4:6
John 15:4-5
Luke 10:1-16
1 Corinthians 9:19-22
Luke 6:27-31
Romans 12:14-20
1 Thessalonians 5:15
1 Peter 3:9
John 8:31-32
Romans 10:1
John 14:6
John 3:16

1 Corinthians 13:6
John 1:12
Romans 10:9
Philippians 3:18
John 8:19
John 5:23, 42-43
Luke 10:16
Matthew 10:40
Mark 7:7
Romans 1:16-17
Galatians 1:6-9
Ephesians 2:8
Revelations 22:19-20
James 1:22-25, 2:26
Philippians 1:3-7
2 Timothy 1:13-14
1 Corinthians 15:1-2
Luke 10:27
Philippians 1:27
Mark 16:15-16
Romans 1:15-16
1 Corinthians 9:16-17
1 Samuel 12:23
Proverbs 3:1-6
Matthew 7:24-27
2 Timothy 2:7-13
Jeremiah 17:5-10

Unconditional Surrender

James 4:7-10
Exodus 3:14
Deuteronomy 6:4
Isaiah 43:10-15
1 Chronicles 29:11-13
John 10:7-12

Revelations 5:11-12
Isaiah 6:1-4
Colossians 2:15
1 Corinthians 10:13
Romans 8:31, 37
Romans 16:19-20
Exodus 9:16
Daniel 4:35
Colossians 1:15-17
2 Corinthians 1:15-17
2 Corinthians 5:10
John 10:10
Jeremiah 29:11-14
John 14:6
Revelations 19:13
John 7:16-18
Exodus 26
Genesis 6:13-22
John 4:34
Romans 8:29
1 Peter 5:8-9
Isaiah 55:8-9
Ephesians 2:1-10

Following after Jesus

1 Peter 2:21
John 8:12
John 14:12
Luke 4:18-20
Luke 22:42
Ephesians 1:7
Matthew 18:18-20
2 Corinthians 6:2
John 3:16-17

A personal relationship with Christ

Revelations 3:20
Jeremiah 29:13
1 Kings 19:12
James 1:19-25
Romans 10:17
John 10:27
Mark 1:35
Psalm 143:8
Psalm 65:4
Psalm 63:1-8
Psalm 92:1-2
Hebrews 10:19-22
John 4:23
Matthew 18:18-20
Matthew 6:9-10
Psalm 66:18-19
Psalm 139:23-24
1 Jon 1:9
Proverbs 28:13
1 Chronicles 29:10-13
Philippians 4:6-7
Psalm 46:10
Isaiah 30:15
Psalm 50:23
Romans 1:21

Continue steadfastly

Acts 2:41-47
Matthew 16:16-18
1 Corinthians 15:6
Acts 2: 42-47
Colossians 1:3-6
Hebrews 13:17

KNOWN BEFORE BIRTH

1 Thessalonians 5:12-13
Ephesians 4:11-13
Acts 6:3
1 Timothy 3
Titus 1
Proverbs 23:19-21, 29-34
Ephesians 5:18
1 Corinthians 1:10
Matthew 12:25
1 Corinthians 12:12-14
Galatians 6:10
Hebrews 10:25
John 14:6
Acts 4:10-12
Matthew 18:20
1 Thessalonians 5:19-24
Galatians 5:22-26
1 Timothy 4:16
Ephesians 5:19-21
Proverbs 6:17-19
Psalm 50:23
John 4:24
Romans 12:1
1 Timothy 4:7-8
Hebrews 11:6
Proverbs 29:18
Luke 10:2-3
Matthew 28:18-20
Titus 2:13-14
1 Peter 4:7-11
Hebrews 12:14
Ecclesiastes 4:9-12
Proverbs 27:17
Hebrews 3:12-13
Mark 4:23-25
Proverbs 13:20

1 John 1:1, 3
1 John 4:19-21
Philippians 2:1-2
1 Corinthians 13:8
John 13:34-35
Matthew 6:9-14

The attitude of a servant

1 John 3:16
John 13:3-17
Romans 1:1
Mark 10:45
Luke 22:27
Ephesians 5:1-2
2 Corinthians 4:5
1 Corinthians 9:19
Romans 6:17-18
Isaiah 53:11
Colossians 3:23
Galatians 5:13
Matthew 25:40
Matthew 10:24
Matthew 24:45-47
Luke 17:7-8
2 Timothy 2:24, 25
Ephesians 6:5-6
Titus 2:9
2 Kings 2:4
2 Samuel 15:21
Luke 12:35-36
Acts 2:16, 18
John 15:4-5
Acts 28:1-3
Luke 9:59-62
Psalm 123:2

Matthew 5:41
Luke 12:37-38
Matthew 25:21
1 Kings 3:8-9
John 12:26

The ministry of giving

Matthew 10:7-8
Matthew 25:40
Acts 3:6
Matthew 6:19-20
Mark 10:21
Philippians 4:17
Hebrews 6:10
Psalm 112:9
Proverbs 19:17
Malachi 3:6-12
Luke 20:25
Proverbs 11:24-25
Proverbs 3:9-10
Acts 2:44-47
Philippians 4:19
Luke 6:38
2 Corinthians 9:6, 7
1 Chronicles 29:9, 17
2 Corinthians 8:12-15
2 Corinthians 9:7
2 Corinthians 8:1-2
Psalm 37:21
Romans 12:8, 13
2 Corinthians 8:2-3
Luke 21:1-4
Matthew 6:1, 3-4
Matthew 25:33-45
James 2:15-16

Ephesians 4:28
Deuteronomy 12:19
Luke 8:3
Galatians 6:6
Philippians 2:25
1 Corinthians 16:2
Acts 20:35
Matthew 5:37
Philippians 3:12-21

Biography

Pieter and JoAnne Bos are the co-founders of: *King's Commission Ministries International.*

They have ministered as Missionaries–Pastor's–Teacher's–Christian Counselor's, Conference Speakers and in the area of Practical Evangelism & Discipleship.

Since 1993, they have taught practical evangelism and discipleship, leadership training, and marriage / family relationship seminars, and preached at "Revival" services throughout the US and over 15 nations worldwide.

They are involved in the area of Church development, and love to encourage the church in the area of church growth, and pursuing a genuine Revival.

Each possesses an unwavering commitment, compassion, and genuineness in their personal lives and ministry..

Their relational ministry style combines solid Preaching and Teaching from God's Word with Mentorship and Equipping.

Pieter and JoAnne have been married over 25 years and have two children, Jamie and Heidi.

Pieter is an ordained minister with the Dutch VPE *(Pentecostal and Evangelical Fellowships),* which is connected to the World Assemblies of God fellowship. And with the Assembly of God in the USA.

Since his arrival in the USA on Dec.1983, Pieter earned a D.Min. *(Practical ministry).* And a Ph.D., *(Christian Counseling).*

Pieter and JoAnne have worked as a team in the ministry of Teen Challenge; as Pastors and Christian Counselors; as Adjunct Professor with *Omega Bible Institute & Seminary, (Omega.edu),* and as Missionary / Teachers.

For more information about the ministry of Pieter and JoAnne Bos visit: www.KingsCommission.Faithweb.com